Sarah Flower, a leading nutritionist and author of many cookery books, is passionate about healthy eating and is a keen advocate of the sugar-free and low-carb way of eating. She has trained with *The Real Meal Revolution*, originally established by Professor Tim Noakes and Jonno Proudfoot, both of whom advise a Banting/LCHF (low-carbohydrate, high-fat) diet and is now herself a Banting coach in the UK. Sarah writes for a number of publications, including the *Daily Mail*, *Top Santé* magazine and *Healthista*. She appears regularly on BBC Radio Devon.

ALSO BY SARAH FLOWER

The Busy Mum's Plan-Ahead Cookbook

The Sugar-Free Family Cookbook

Eat Well, Spend Less

The Healthy Lifestyle Diet Cookbook

The Healthy Halogen Cookbook

The Healthy Slow Cooker Cookbook

Perfect Baking with Your Halogen Oven

Halogen Cooking for Two

The Everyday Halogen Family Cookbook

The Everyday Halogen Oven Cookbook

Slow Cook, Fast Food

Low-Carb Slow Cooker

Eating to Beat Type 2 Diabetes

Slow Cooker Family Classics

The Keto Slow Cooker

Slow Cooker for Less

Comfort Food

FROM
YOUR SLOW COOKER

SIMPLE RECIPES
TO MAKE YOU FEEL GOOD

SARAH FLOWER

ROBINSON

ROBINSON

First published in Great Britain in 2022 by Robinson

Copyright © Sarah Flower, 2022

10 9 8 7 6 5 4 3 2

A CIP catalogue record for this book is available from the British Library.

ISBN 978-1-47214-773-8

Designed by Thextension

Illustrations adapted from those by Iryn © Shutterstock

Typeset in Bely, Bely Display and Silka

Printed and bound in Great Britain by Bell & Bain Ltd, Glasgow

Papers used by Robinson are from well-managed forests and other responsible sources.

Robinson
An imprint of Little, Brown Book Group
Carmelite House, 50 Victoria Embankment, London EC4Y 0DZ

An Hachette UK Company

www.hachette.co.uk

www.littlebrown.co.uk

The recommendations given in this book are solely intended as education and should not be taken as medical advice.

Contents

3 Beef

4 Pork

8 Side Dishes

9 Desserts

Introduction

I wrote my first slow cooker book in 2010. My second slow cooker book, *The Healthy Slow Cooker Cookbook*, was published two years later, and, thankfully, it is still selling well. This will be my seventh slow cooker book, out of more than twenty books to date. This book is all about comfort: comforting food, but also comfort in terms of being stress free. While this is not a health book, cooking from scratch is one of the best ways to cook, and slow cooking helps to preserve the nutrients in foods. The recipes in this book do not aim to keep calories or fat and sugar content low, although in the desserts chapter I do suggest options to reduce sugar.

I have a very busy home life alongside my clinical work as a nutritionist, writing books and media work, as well as teaching, so my slow cooker gets used an awful lot. Slow cookers really do make our lives so much easier. You can prepare all the ingredients in the morning, turn the slow cooker on and leave your meal to cook while you are working or getting on with your busy day, then come home to a nourishing meal. Effortless – and far, far better for us than any processed ready meal!

The desserts chapter – one of my favourites – is full of classic family recipes, some of which you may recognise from your childhood. I have not tweaked these to make them healthier, but if you read the opening paragraphs of the chapter, you will find my top tips on how to convert these recipes to fit your dietary requirements, with tweaks for sugar-free, vegan and gluten-free diets.

One thing I really want to stress: please read the technical chapters, especially if you are new to the slow cooker. It is really important to get to know your slow cooker. Some can cook differently to others, especially if your machine is slightly older or maybe a cheaper variety. You need the slow cooker lid to form a good seal, to prevent evaporation. You also need to ensure your slow cooker does not overheat. You don't want to be boiling everything at a fast simmer, evaporating the liquid. This can affect the timings and heat settings. The idea is slow, low and long. My suggestions are only guidelines, so if you are unsure opt only for the low settings until you get to know your machine.

If you are new to a machine, my top tip is to buy a multi-cooker that switches from a sauté/hob facility to slow cooker, as this will make your life so much easier. Also ensure it has a timer that switches to warm once the set time has been reached. This is important if you are late home; you don't want to come home to a bowl of mush instead of your lovely casserole. If your slow cooker doesn't have this option, you can invest in a timing plug, which will at least ensure you are cooking things only for the suggested times.

I do hope you enjoy this book. If you do, maybe you would like to get in touch. It is always lovely to hear from readers. You can contact me by visiting my website at www.sarahflower.co.uk or via Twitter and Instagram @MsSarahFlower. I will also be sharing recipes and cookery videos on my Facebook pages: *HealthySlowCooker* and *EverydaySugarFree*.

I hope you enjoy the recipes and the delicious meals you are about to create!

Sarah x

How to use your slow cooker

Slow cookers gained popularity in the 1970s, but the principle of slow cooking goes back hundreds of years – think of the large stock pots seen dangling from ranges! Slow cookers were seen to revolutionise the kitchen; they could create wholesome meals ready for your return after a busy day. They were incredibly popular, but sadly became relegated to kitchen cupboards as we moved into a faster pace of life, where processed and convenience foods took over and, for some, the need to live a frugal life became less relevant. Cheaper cuts of meats were no longer popular, so there seemed to be no real reason to keep the slow cooker in our kitchens. The microwave and processed food became the housewife's choice for a busy home, and the poor slow cooker ceased to inspire. Thankfully we are now seeing a revival as we realise that not only can these clever machines save us time, but they can also offer us superior nutrition.

▶ ▶ ▶

You can buy slow cookers from as little as £15, and we are now seeing multi-cookers, of which I am a huge fan, increase in popularity too. When purchasing a slow cooker or multi-cooker, it is important to consider how it is going to be used. Think about the size of the machine. Outwardly, some might look quite big, but the size of the stock pot itself may not be as large as you need. If you are cooking for a large family or like to plan ahead and freeze food, you may be better off spending more money and investing in a larger machine. Go to an electrical store where you can view the machines – even if you don't buy from them, it will give you an idea of the range of machines on sale and what your requirements are. I would also strongly recommend you buy the best you can afford.

These are the functions I absolutely love:

✳ Multi-function: This basically means I can switch from sauté to slow cooker all in one machine. This saves time and washing-up (which is a win-win for me).

✳ Timers: I feel these are absolutely vital. My machine allows me to set a cooking time in high or low. Once that set time has been reached, it then switches to warm, ensuring my food does not spoil.

✳ Auto: Some machines have an auto button. This basically means a machine will start off on high and, once the temperature has been reached, will switch down to low.

KNOW YOUR OWN MACHINE

This is really important! Every machine is different, and if you are buying one for the first time, I would recommend you purchase one with a timing switch so it can turn itself to warm once the set time has been reached – this avoids any possible disasters with overcooking. As mentioned above, some newer machines will have an auto button or switch that turns the machine onto high until the desired temperature is reached, then switches to low. Most will have a high and a low setting.

If you have an old machine, check if its temperature remains accurate. If you suspect it is running too hot, you can use an oven thermometer to check. Machines can vary, but most aim to function at around 77°C on low and 90°C on high. Some can get much hotter, which can result in burning on the base or around the edges when left on high for long periods. If you are worried, use your machine only on low. The temperature should not create a boil; it should be a low, slow cook and not a fast, boiling cook.

MULTI-COOKERS

As a massive fan of the slow cooker, I thought I knew all there is to know about these machines, but that was until I discovered the multi-cooker. Initially I thought it was a bit of a gimmick – stating it can steam, slow cook, roast, sauté and bake – but it has won me over. I have reviewed several of these machines, but a Crockpot Multi-Cooker has now taken pride of place on my kitchen worktop.

Some slow cookers do have a sauté option, but I have found these a bit hit and miss. However, the multi-cooker really is an all-in-one cooking experience. The sauté option allows you to sauté with five different temperature settings. The slow cooker function allows you to choose from high, low and warm. Once the cooking time has been reached it automatically switches to warm mode. Perfect if you are late home for dinner! The roasting rack can be used either low or high depending on the size of your joint. I cooked a small joint of beef, sealing first with the sauté facility, before adding some vegetables to the base, popping my beef joint on top and switching to roast for 45 minutes. It cooked perfectly, and the vegetables and juices at the base made a delicious stock. I allowed the beef to rest, washed out the crock-pot bowl, added some water to the base and steamed my vegetables in minutes. So easy!

TO SAUTÉ OR NOT TO SAUTÉ?

Recipes often tell you to sauté the onions or brown the meat. I have tried with and without, and, to be honest, I really didn't notice much difference in the taste, but if you do sauté, the colour is more appealing and it also helps to seal the meat. If you are cooking a whole chicken, for example, remember that it will not brown, so may look a bit unappealing. Sautéing the chicken, as well as adding colour, also stops it from flaking into the dish. Coating meat with a low-carb, grain-free flour can also help if you want a thicker sauce – remember the slow cooker does not lose that much liquid, so you may find you need to thicken the dish until you get used to the way your machine works – they are all different! All multi-cookers offer a sauté option. You may find that your slow cooker has a sauté facility too; others come with hob-proof dishes, allowing you to transfer from one heat source to the other. For more information, you will need to refer to the manufacturer's instructions for your particular machine. Where applicable, a recipe will detail both techniques, allowing you to choose which you prefer.

COOKING TECHNIQUES

All slow cookers come with full manufacturer's instructions, recipe suggestions and even a useful helpline you can call if you get stuck. I strongly advise you to read these booklets before using your machine. Here are some reminders:

✳ Some cookers need to be preheated, which can take up to 15 minutes. Others heat up fast so you may not need to preheat them (refer to your manufacturer's recommendations).

✳ As a general rule of thumb, one hour in a conventional oven equates to two to three hours on high in a slow cooker, or six hours on low heat. Some slow cookers have an auto setting – this basically means that they heat up quickly on high, then when the set temperature has been reached, revert to low for the remainder of the cooking time; this helps the food, especially meat, reach a safe temperature quickly. Some machines have a warm setting, which is useful if the food has reached its maximum cooking time and you are just wanting to keep it warm, but really the low setting is enough, and food can cook for ten hours without starting to spoil.

✳ You may need to adjust the liquid content of your dish depending on your personal taste, but remember that you do need liquid in order to cook the food and that all food must be submersed in liquid before cooking. Potatoes especially may bob around on top and go black, so push them into the stock. Your manufacturer's guidelines should detail the minimum and maximum fill levels for your machine. The slow cooker does not evaporate liquid as much as other cooking methods, so you may need to thicken soups or casseroles. Adding more water or stock is simple and can be done at any stage. If you find your slow cooker does evaporate liquid, it may be overheating.

✳ The key point to remember about slow cooking is that once you've set your machine off cooking, you shouldn't keep removing the lid as this reduces the temperature and it will then take longer for the slow cooker to get back up to the required temperature. The outer edge of the lid forms a seal – sometimes this may spit or bubble out, but this is quite normal. Only remove it when absolutely essential, ideally when cooking is finished or, if necessary, in the last 30 minutes of cooking to add key ingredients. If you are the sort of person who likes to keep an eye on things, opt for a slow cooker with a glass lid (though this is not foolproof as they do get steamed up!).

✳ Always defrost any frozen ingredients thoroughly before placing them in the slow cooker, especially meat. The slow cooker is designed to cook safely at low temperatures, however, if your cooker does not maintain the required heat, this could increase the risk of food poisoning caused by the spread of bacteria. Frozen foods such as peas, sweetcorn, prawns and other quick-cook vegetables should be added only in the last 30 minutes of cooking time.

✶ When adding liquids such as stock or water, in order to maintain the temperature it is better to use warm liquids (not boiling) rather than cold.

✶ Pasta should be added only in the last 30 minutes of cooking time as it goes very soggy and breaks up during longer cooking times.

✶ Fresh herbs can be used but tend to lose their intensity of flavour over longer cooking times. If I am using these, I add them in the last 30 minutes of cooking.

✶ Vegetables, especially root vegetables, take much longer to cook than meat. You can speed up the process by sautéing the vegetables prior to adding to the dish, or by simply chopping them into smaller chunks. Make sure the vegetables are thoroughly immersed in the stock, ideally near the base as this is the hottest area.

CAKES

I have made cakes in the slow cooker, and these have been really tasty, though sometimes they can have a different texture to oven-baked cakes. I think it is a question of personal taste. Some people may not like the moist, almost bread pudding-like texture of the fruit cakes. I have cooked cakes simply by placing a cake dish in the slow cooker and adding water to the base to create a bain-marie, which works well with sponge puddings and Christmas pudding.

FREEZING

If you want to get ahead, why not double up the recipe and freeze some? If you are going to do this, make sure you remove the dish from the slow cooker and allow it to chill thoroughly before freezing. You can buy special freezer bags for more liquid-heavy meals such as soups or casseroles. Make sure the food is completely defrosted before reheating.

CONVERSION CHARTS

WEIGHT

Metric	Imperial
25g	1oz
50g	2oz
75g	3oz
100g	4oz
150g	5oz
175g	6oz
200g	7oz
225g	8oz
250g	9oz
300g	10oz
350g	12oz
400g	14oz
450g	1lb

LIQUIDS

Metric	Imperial	US cup
5ml	1 tsp	1 tsp
15ml	1 tbsp	1 tbsp
50ml	2fl oz	3 tbsp
60ml	2½fl oz	¼ cup
75ml	3fl oz	⅓ cup
100ml	4fl oz	scant ½ cup
125ml	4½fl oz	½ cup
150ml	5fl oz	⅔ cup
200ml	7fl oz	scant 1 cup
250ml	9fl oz	1 cup
300ml	½ pint	1¼ cups
350ml	12fl oz	1⅓ cups
400ml	¾ pint	1¾ cups
500ml	17fl oz	2 cups
600ml	1 pt	2½ cups

MEASUREMENTS

Metric	Imperial
5cm	2in
10cm	4in
13cm	5in
15cm	6in
18cm	7in
20cm	8in
25cm	10in
30cm	12in

SYMBOLS

Double up & freeze

Vegetarian

Vegan

Dairy free option

1

Soups are bursting with nutrients. Quick and easy to prepare, they can be used as a snack or a nutritious meal. Soups are a great way of getting extra vegetables into your family's diet. They are also cheap to make and very filling. Best of all, as they are slow-cooked at a low temperature, this means that the nutrients are maintained, which makes the soup ultra-healthy. If you or your child takes a packed lunch, why not invest in a small flask and fill it with your home-made soup? Perfect to fill up and warm the body, especially during the winter months. Most soups can be frozen, so fill your freezer with individual portions ready for lunches.

SOUP-MAKING ADVICE

STOCK

Stock cubes can be quite overpowering, and some can be high in salt and/or sugar, but there are some great products available now that give a more natural flavour. I use my own stock, but I also really like using gel stocks for added flavour. Home-made stock is packed with nutrients, particularly if you use animal bones. I am a huge fan of bone stock as it is packed with nutrients. You can freeze this stock, so make it in batches. ▶ ▶ ▶

PURÉEING SOUPS

Some people like a chunky soup; others prefer a smooth soup. It is purely down to personal taste. When puréeing a soup, I use an electric hand blender (some people call it a stick blender). It is simple to use and saves on washing-up and messy transfer to a liquidiser, though do make sure the end of the blender is fully submerged in the soup or you will end up with it everywhere! For a smooth soup, you can filter through a sieve.

CHUNKY SOUPS

Some chunky soups may benefit from a thicker stock/sauce. To achieve this, simply remove about a quarter of the soup and purée or liquidise it, then add it back to the soup.

LIQUID – THICK OR THIN

You may need to adjust the liquid content of your soup depending on your personal taste. The slow cooker does not evaporate liquid as much as other cooking methods so you may need to thicken soups. If you find your slow cooker is evaporating liquid excessively and therefore likely to be cooking too hot, my advice would be to cook everything on low.

Here are my top tips to thicken soups or casseroles:

1 Remove the lid of the slow cooker and allow the steam to evaporate, which helps to reduce the liquid.

2 Mix a couple of teaspoons of cornflour with cold water and, once mixed, pour into the slow cooker and stir well.

3 Remove some of the chunky soup and purée or liquidise it before mixing it back into the slow cooker.

4 Add a handful of red lentils and cook on high for 30 minutes.

PULSES AND BEANS
Adding pulses and beans is a cheap way to bulk out a meal, and it also adds essential nutrients to your dish and can keep you feeling fuller for longer.

CREAMS
Creams, milk, Greek yoghurt and crème fraîche can sometimes separate when cooked in a slow cooker for long periods so it's best to add these just before serving.

VEGAN AND VEGETARIAN
Some of the recipes that follow contain cream, but if you are vegan, you can swap this for coconut cream.

CREAMY SPICED LENTIL SOUP

SERVES 4

NUTRITIONAL INFORMATION PER SERVING

437 Kcals

19g fat

43g net carbohydrates

16g protein

INGREDIENTS

1 onion, finely chopped

2 garlic cloves, crushed

3cm piece fresh ginger, peeled and finely chopped

1 red pepper, deseeded and finely chopped

2 tbsp mild curry powder, or to taste

1 tsp ground turmeric

3 tomatoes, finely chopped

200g red lentils

2 tbsp tomato purée

400g tin coconut milk

500ml vegetable stock (or chicken stock, if preferred)

salt and ground black pepper

chopped red chillies and chopped coriander, to garnish

This is so easy to make and costs very little. It is the perfect comfort lunch for all the family. This version is mild and creamy, but you can make it spicier by adding a few chopped chillies and using a stronger curry powder. Serve with some lovely toasted naan or flatbreads.

1 Preheat your slow cooker following the manufacturer's instructions.

2 Add all the ingredients and stir well until combined. Season to taste.

3 Cook on low for 6–8 hours.

4 You can add more stock if needed, depending on the consistency you prefer.

5 Garnish with chopped red chillies and coriander.

6 Serve with naan or flatbreads.

TOMATO, RED PEPPER & MASCARPONE SOUP

SERVES 4–6

I love this soup. It has a wonderful flavour but is also comfort in a bowl. It is a far richer and more nutritious take on a traditional tomato soup. I add red lentils to boost the nutrient content of the meal. I use fresh tomatoes in this soup, but you can use a very good quality tinned tomato, such as cherry tomatoes, which gives a far nicer flavour.

1 Preheat your slow cooker following the manufacturer's instructions.

2 Add all the ingredients apart from the mascarpone and combine well. Season to taste.

3 Cook on low for 5–6 hours.

4 Stir in the mascarpone. Use an electric hand blender to whizz until smooth. Add stock if the soup is too thick. Reheat for another 15 minutes.

5 Serve garnished with chopped basil or a swirl of cream.

TO MAKE IT VEGAN AND DAIRY-FREE

Swap the mascarpone for coconut cream.

NUTRITIONAL INFORMATION PER SERVING

410 Kcals

26g fat

22g net carbohydrates

8.3g protein

INGREDIENTS

1 large onion, finely diced

1 garlic clove, finely chopped

6 fresh tomatoes, chopped (or 2 x 400g tins chopped tomatoes)

100g red lentils, washed

2 tbsp sundried tomato paste

1 red pepper, finely diced

1 tsp oregano

½ tsp dried basil

200ml vegetable stock

300g mascarpone

seasoning, to taste

chopped basil or swirl of cream, to garnish

BUTTERNUT, SWEET POTATO & CARROT SOUP

SERVES 4

NUTRITIONAL INFORMATION
PER SERVING

135 Kcals

1.8g fat

26g net carbohydrates

2.8g protein

INGREDIENTS

1 onion, diced

2 garlic cloves, crushed

2 red chillies, diced

3cm piece fresh ginger, roughly chopped

1 stick celery, diced

150g butternut squash, deseeded, peeled and diced

1 sweet potato, peeled and diced

2 medium carrots, diced

1 tsp ground coriander

½ tsp ground cumin

1 tsp chilli powder

1 tsp thyme

1 tsp sumac

550ml vegetable stock, warm

seasoning, to taste

swirl of cream or yoghurt

sprinkle of paprika or chopped chillies and spring onions, to garnish

A wonderful winter warmer full of antioxidants. These vegetables work perfectly with chilli, as you need its kick to offset the rather mellow creamy flavours. You can of course tone this down if you prefer, but don't be afraid of the chilli – it does mellow out when cooked.

1 Preheat your slow cooker following the manufacturer's instructions.

2 Chop all your vegetables and add to the slow cooker.

3 Add the spices, cover with warm stock and season to taste.

4 Cook on low for 6–7 hours.

5 When ready, taste to check the seasoning before liquidising (I use an electric hand blender rather than transferring to a liquidiser as this saves on the washing-up!). You can adjust the thickness if you need to, by adding more stock or boiling water to thin it down.

6 To serve, place the soup in serving bowls, add a swirl of cream or yoghurt in the centre of the soup and garnish with a sprinkle of paprika or chopped chillies and spring onions.

WINTER VEGETABLE & QUINOA SOUP

SERVES 4

A wholesome soup, perfect for a winter's day or when you fancy something a bit more filling, this is great for using up any vegetables you may have – although I would avoid swede as it can be very overpowering in a soup. This is a chunky soup, so cut all your vegetables into equal bite-size pieces, to ensure an even cook.

1 Preheat your slow cooker following the manufacturer's instructions.

2 Rinse the quinoa well before placing into the slow cooker. Add all the remaining ingredients apart from the spinach.

3 Cook on low for 5–6 hours or high for 3–4 hours.

4 Thirty minutes before serving, add the spinach, stirring it in well to allow it to submerge into the soup. Turn to high and continue to cook for the remaining 30 minutes.

5 Serve in bowls with chunky bread topped with hummus.

NUTRITIONAL INFORMATION PER SERVING

270 Kcals

2.9g fat

48g net carbohydrates

8.6g protein

INGREDIENTS

150g quinoa

1 onion, finely chopped

2 garlic cloves, finely chopped

1 carrot, diced

2 sticks celery, diced

1 sweet potato, diced

1 leek, finely chopped

1 small parsnip, diced

650ml vegetable stock

1 tsp paprika

1 tsp marjoram

1 bay leaf

1 tsp dried parsley

seasoning, to taste

60g baby leaf spinach

RIBOLLITA

NUTRITIONAL INFORMATION PER SERVING

303 Kcals

4.7g fat

45g net carbohydrates

13g protein

INGREDIENTS

1 onion, diced

2–3 garlic cloves, crushed

2 sticks celery, diced

1 large carrot, diced

1 small potato, peeled and diced (optional)

400g tin chopped tomatoes

1 tbsp sundried tomato paste

2 x 400g tins cannellini beans (or other beans), drained

90g pearl barley, rinsed (omit if making gluten-free)

pinch chilli flakes (plus some for garnish)

650ml vegetable or chicken stock

2 bay leaves

½ tsp smoked paprika

1 tsp chilli powder (optional)

seasoning, to taste

100g kale, chopped (or use spinach or cavolo nero if you prefer)

NOTE

When dicing the veg, ensure the pieces are evenly sized.

This is a delicious, very nutritious and filling Tuscan-style soup, traditionally made with leftovers such as beans and vegetables. You can adopt the same leftover principle and add ingredients to suit your store cupboard and fridge. I tend to use cannellini beans in mine, with either kale, spinach or cavolo nero, but you can swap the beans for whatever you have in the cupboard.

1 Preheat your slow cooker following the manufacturer's instructions.

2 Place all the ingredients into your slow cooker apart from the kale and stir well until combined.

3 Cook on low for 6–8 hours.

4 Thirty minutes before serving, add the kale.

5 Serve with a sprinkle of chilli flakes.

CHILLI, RED LENTIL, TOMATO & COCONUT SOUP

SERVES 4

This is a filling and warming soup. You can omit the chilli if you don't like the heat, but I would highly recommend it. This soup is delicious when drizzled with a little cream or coconut cream before serving.

1 Preheat your slow cooker following the manufacturer's instructions.

2 Add all the ingredients and combine well. Season to taste.

3 Cook on low for 5–6 hours.

4 You can leave the soup as it is or, if you prefer a more creamed consistency, you can use an electric hand blender and whizz until smooth. Add stock if the soup is too thick.

5 To serve, add a swirl of cream or coconut cream to taste and garnish with chopped coriander and chopped chillies.

NUTRITIONAL INFORMATION PER SERVING

381 Kcals

22g fat

30g net carbohydrates

11g protein

INGREDIENTS

1 large onion, finely diced

1 garlic clove, finely chopped

1–2 chillies, to taste

3cm piece fresh ginger, grated

1 tbsp garam masala

6 tomatoes, chopped

100g lentils, washed

1 tbsp tomato purée

1 red pepper, finely diced

400g tin coconut milk

2 tbsp desiccated coconut

100–250ml vegetable, bone or chicken stock

1 tsp ground turmeric

seasoning, to taste

swirl of cream or coconut cream

chopped coriander and chopped chillies, to garnish

CREAMY MUSHROOM SOUP

SERVES 4

NUTRITIONAL INFORMATION PER SERVING

449 Kcals

38g fat

15g net carbohydrates

7.6g protein

INGREDIENTS

500g white mushrooms

30g dried porcini mushrooms

1 large onion, finely chopped

2 garlic cloves, finely chopped

2 tbsp dry sherry

300ml vegetable stock (or chicken, if preferred)

1 tsp thyme

½ tsp tarragon

seasoning, to taste (I use plenty of black pepper)

300ml double cream

juice of ½ lemon

1–2 tbsp cornflour (if needed)

30–50ml water (if needed)

fresh parsley leaves, to garnish

This is a traditional-style mushroom soup, ideally made with chestnut or button mushrooms. For added depth of flavour, I have added some rehydrated porcini mushrooms. If you are vegetarian, you can use vegetable stock, but I use my own chicken stock to add more depth of flavour.

1 Preheat your slow cooker following the manufacturer's instructions.

2 Soak the porcini mushrooms in boiling water until rehydrated.

3 Add all the ingredients apart from the cream and lemon juice. Combine well and season to taste.

4 Cook on low for 4 hours.

5 Use an electric hand blender to whizz up the mushrooms while in the slow cooker until you have formed a smooth soup. Add the cream and the lemon juice. Season to taste again if needed. Combine well.

6 If you want to thicken the soup, mix 1–2 tablespoons of cornflour with 30–50ml water to form a paste, add to the slow cooker and combine well.

7 Place back on low heat for another hour.

8 Serve with a garnish of fresh parsley leaves.

ASPARAGUS SOUP

SERVES 4

Asparagus is great for our health, providing a good source of folate, and also supports a healthy gut. Serve this soup with some rustic home-made bread.

1 Preheat your slow cooker following the manufacturer's instructions.

2 Place the asparagus and onion in your slow cooker. Add the stock and wine, and season to taste with black pepper.

3 Place on high and cook for 1½–2 hours. Add the baby leaf spinach and cook on high for another 30 minutes.

4 Use an electric hand blender to whizz the soup while in the slow cooker until it forms a smooth soup.

5 Garnish with chopped sesame seeds before serving.

NUTRITIONAL INFORMATION
PER SERVING

91 Kcals

0.9g fat

8.1g net carbohydrates

4.8g protein

INGREDIENTS

500g asparagus stalks, chopped

1 onion, finely chopped

300ml vegetable stock
(or chicken, if preferred)

150ml white wine

black pepper

80g baby leaf spinach

Chicken is one of the most popular meat choices in the UK. It works well in the slow cooker but does not need the long, slow cook required by tougher kinds of meat, such as lamb or beef.

Most families opt for chicken breast, but for slow cooking and enhanced flavour, I would recommend using thighs and leg meat as these are much better suited to longer cooks and have the added bonus of often being much cheaper to buy. You can buy these cuts skinless and boneless so they're suitable for all the family to enjoy.

If you are roasting a chicken for Sunday lunch, buy a size bigger and use the leftover meat – from all over the chicken, not just the breast and legs – to make yourself a chicken pie, chicken crumble, chicken fajitas or enchiladas, or even a curry. Don't forget to save the bones. They make an excellent and very nourishing chicken stock.

POACHING CHICKEN

If you are fed up with dried chicken cooked in the oven, you can use your slow cooker to poach it. This is a great method if you want lovely tender chicken for salads or sandwiches. Simply add your chicken breasts or thighs to the slow cooker, cover with chicken stock, and cook on low for 4–5 hours or on high for 2–3 hours. Remove the chicken from the stock, but retain the stock, which can be put in the fridge or frozen to use for another dish.

BUTTERFLYING CHICKEN

You will be asked to butterfly chicken breasts in the recipe for Bacon-Wrapped Chicken with Mushrooms & Cheese Stuffing (page 48). To do so, place your hand over the breast and, using a very sharp knife, carefully cut horizontally, but do not cut completely – you must stop before you reach the edge as you want the breast to open like butterfly wings or the pages of a book.

1 Cover the chicken with cling film and, using a wooden kitchen mallet or wooden rolling pin, bash it lightly until you have a flat butterfly shape. This makes it much easier if you want to stuff and roll the chicken.

2 Once stuffed and rolled, you can hold the chicken together with a wooden cocktail stick.

CREATING A CHICKEN POCKET

Another option if you want to stuff chicken is to create a pocket. This is great if you want to stuff it with a few slices of mozzarella or similar.

1 Using a very sharp knife, cut into the thickest part of the chicken breast, making a cut about 4–5cm long to create a pocket – make sure you do not cut through.

2 Once you have stuffed the chicken you can hold it together with a wooden cocktail stick to stop the stuffing coming out.

CREAMY BACON, MUSHROOM & THYME CHICKEN

SERVES 4

NUTRITIONAL INFORMATION PER SERVING

533 Kcals

39g fat

8.5g net carbohydrates

30g protein

INGREDIENTS

2–3 garlic cloves

1 small onion, finely chopped

150g smoked pancetta or lardons, diced

500g skinless, boneless chicken fillets (leg, thigh or breast)

150ml white wine

250ml chicken stock

1 chicken gel stock cube

1 tsp dried thyme

1 tbsp cornflour

50ml water

200ml double cream

80g chestnut mushrooms, sliced

seasoning, to taste

chopped parsley, to garnish

I developed this recipe when I first started working with clients on a low-carb diet in clinic. It very quickly became a meal my family enjoyed on an almost weekly basis. The reviews are amazing for this – it is so tasty. You can make this on the hob (I use a heavy sauté pan), but it also works well in the slow cooker. I serve this with steamed green vegetables; there's no need for additional carbs in the form of potatoes or rice, as the protein and fat combo will really fill you up.

1 Preheat your slow cooker following the manufacturer's instructions.

2 Place the garlic, onion, pancetta, chicken, wine, stock, gel stock cube and thyme into the slow cooker.

3 Cook on low for 6 hours. If you want it faster, you can cook on high for 3–4 hours.

4 Thirty minutes before serving, mix the cornflour with 50ml cold water to form a paste. Add this to the slow cooker, along with the cream and mushrooms.

5 Season to taste.

6 Cook for a further thirty minutes on high.

7 Garnish with chopped parsley and serve with steamed green vegetables.

NOTE

If you want to brown the chicken, you can do this before adding to the slow cooker. Simply heat some oil in a sauté pan and brown the chicken before placing into your slow cooker. Although this step is purely for aesthetics, so is not strictly necessary.

RUSTIC COQ AU VIN

SERVES 4

A quick and easy variation on the traditional French favourite. I cook this with the skin on and always opt for thighs. When you use chicken with the skin on, it really does need to be browned well before you add it to the slow cooker, for aesthetics as well as taste. If you prefer not to use chicken with the skin on, you can miss out the browning stage.

1 Preheat your slow cooker following the manufacturer's instructions.

2 In a bowl, mix together the flour, paprika and black pepper.

3 Dip the chicken into the flour mix before adding to a hot, oiled sauté pan. If you have a multi-cooker, you can use this on the sauté setting. If you are not using thighs with skin on, you can omit this step. Add the lardons and cook a little until it starts to brown. Remove from heat.

4 Add all the ingredients to the slow cooker apart from the mushrooms. Season to taste. Make sure the stock is hot when you add it as this will keep the temperature.

5 Cook on low for 6–7 hours.

6 One hour before serving, add the mushrooms, ensuring they are submerged into the stock.

7 Remove the bay leaves before serving.

8 Serve with mashed potatoes and steamed green vegetables.

NUTRITIONAL INFORMATION PER SERVING

485 Kcals

13g fat

21g net carbohydrates

37g protein

INGREDIENTS

2 tbsp flour

1 tsp paprika

black pepper, to taste

500g chicken thighs or legs with skin on (thighs and legs give nicer flavour than breasts, skin is optional)

1 tbsp olive oil (if browning)

200g smoked bacon (cooking bacon is also good), thickly diced

12 shallots, whole

3–4 garlic cloves, roughly chopped

2 sticks celery, sliced

250ml red wine

200ml port

50ml brandy

2 chicken gel stock cubes

2 bay leaves

2–3 sprigs thyme

seasoning, to taste

200g button mushrooms, halved or quartered

BACON-WRAPPED CHICKEN WITH MUSHROOMS & CHEESE STUFFING

SERVES 4

NUTRITIONAL INFORMATION PER SERVING

417 Kcals

26g fat

1.3 net carbohydrates

45g protein

INGREDIENTS

4 chicken breasts (approx. 600g)

150g mature Cheddar cheese, grated

80g chestnut mushroom, sliced

2 garlic cloves, crushed

small handful fresh basil

seasoning, to taste

200g back or streaky bacon

300ml chicken or bone stock (or you can use white wine if preferred)

This is one of the most perfect flavour combinations – ultimate comfort. Cheese, chicken, bacon and mushrooms – what's not to like? You can prepare these in advance and store in the fridge until you are ready to add them to the slow cooker. The bacon will be pale so you may prefer to place under the grill for a few minutes before serving to help crisp and colour it.

1 Preheat your slow cooker following the manufacturer's instructions.

2 Butterfly the chicken breast using a very sharp knife (see page 42 for more information). Start at the thickest edge and work to the thinnest, being careful not to cut through – you want the chicken to fold open like the wings of a butterfly. You can then open the chicken breast. If it is uneven, just bash it a little with a wooden rolling pin until it forms a flat butterfly ready for you to stuff and roll.

3 Place a generous layer of cheese, mushroom, garlic and basil in the middle of the chicken breasts. Carefully roll up the chicken breast. Cover the chicken with the rashers of bacon, using them to help wrap and secure it. You can secure with a wooden cocktail stick if you prefer, otherwise when you come to put them into the slow cooker, place the bacon-wrapped breast rolls seam-down.

4 Once they are all complete, pour the chicken stock into the slow cooker and place the chicken on the top. Season to taste.

5 Cook on low for 4–5 hours until cooked through.

6 If you want to brown the bacon, you can place the rolls under the grill until golden and crispy before serving.

7 Finish with a drizzle of the stock and serve with mashed potato and steamed vegetables.

ASIAN-INSPIRED CHICKEN

SERVES 4

This is an easy take on Asian sticky chicken. It is a quick bung-it-all-in type of meal, but tastes impressive, despite the little work it needs. Don't forget to top with sesame seeds and sliced spring onions as this really makes the dish come to life on the plate. I serve with fluffy white rice or, when watching the carbs, cauliflower rice.

1 Preheat your slow cooker following the manufacturer's instructions.

2 Place the chicken and onion in the slow cooker with the garlic, chilli and ginger.

3 In a jug, mix the rice wine vinegar, honey, brown sugar, sweet chilli sauce, tomato purée and soy sauce. Once combined, pour this onto the chicken and combine well.

4 Cook on low for 4–5 hours. You can cook on high for 2–3 hours, but if doing so, line the slow cooker or place the mixture in an ovenproof dish inside the slow cooker as the sugary sauce can sometimes catch on the slow cooker and burn or stick when on high, especially in some older machines.

5 When ready to serve, finish with a garnish of sesame seeds and spring onions.

6 Serve on a bed of rice.

NUTRITIONAL INFORMATION PER SERVING

278 Kcals

3.7g fat

26g net carbohydrates

34g protein

INGREDIENTS

700g skinless, boneless chicken thigh or breast fillets, diced

1 onion, finely diced

3 garlic cloves, crushed

2 red chillies, finely chopped

3cm piece fresh ginger, grated

1 tbsp rice wine vinegar

2 tbsp runny honey

2 tbsp brown sugar

3 tbsp sweet chilli sauce

2 tbsp tomato purée

4 tbsp soy sauce

small handful sesame seeds, to garnish

3–4 spring onions, finely chopped, to garnish

CHICKEN ROGAN JOSH

SERVES 4

NUTRITIONAL INFORMATION
PER SERVING

476 Kcals

36g fat

9.9g net carbohydrates

27g protein

INGREDIENTS

1 tsp cumin seeds

1 tsp fennel seeds, crushed

4 green cardamom pods, crushed

1 tbsp olive oil

3 garlic cloves, crushed

2 red chillies, diced (deseed first if you prefer a mellower flavour)

1 tsp asafoetida

1 tsp ground ginger

2 tsp Kashmiri chilli powder

2 tsp garam masala

500g skinless, boneless chicken thigh or breast fillets

200g carton creamed coconut

400g tin chopped tomatoes

4–6 cherry tomatoes, halved (optional)

2–3 spring onions, sliced, to garnish

This is my take on a traditional rogan josh and a recipe my family really enjoys. Do not underestimate the importance of the spices – this is why I always have a variety of good-quality spices in my store cupboard – and ensure they are in date as they do lose their potency as they age. You can buy a ready-made rogan josh blend, but I urge you to invest in the separate spices as it really does make a huge difference.

1 Preheat your slow cooker following the manufacturer's instructions.

2 Grind your cumin and fennel seeds along with the cardamom pods in a pestle and mortar.

3 Place the olive oil in a sauté pan (if your slow cooker has a sauté facility you can use this instead of a separate pan). Add the garlic, chillies and spices, and allow to cook on a medium heat for 2–3 minutes until the spices start to become more fragrant.

4 Add the chicken and coat until it is white, to seal. If you have been using a sauté pan, transfer the chicken to the slow cooker.

5 Add the coconut cream and tinned tomatoes. Combine well.

6 Cook on low for 6–8 hours. Just before serving, stir in the cherry tomatoes (if using).

7 Garnish with sliced spring onions.

8 Serve with basmati or pilau rice and flatbreads.

NOTE

Coconut cream can usually be found in small cartons near the Asian cuisine sections of large supermarkets. Do not confuse it with creamed coconut block, the solid type that you have to soften before use. If you don't have coconut cream, place tinned coconut milk in the fridge, which will allow the cream to harden so you can scoop it off without adding the extra water content to the dish.

CREAMY CHICKEN WITH SUNDRIED TOMATOES & SPINACH

SERVES 4

I am a big fan of creamy dishes, and this one is no exception. It works brilliantly in the slow cooker. If I fancy shaking up the recipe, I sometimes add chorizo instead of the pancetta. Perfect served with some steamed vegetables.

1 Place the garlic, onion, pancetta, chicken, wine, stock and gel stock cube into the slow cooker.

2 Cook on low for 6 hours. If you want it to cook faster, you can place it on high for 3–4 hours.

3 Thirty minutes before serving, mix the cornflour with 50ml cold water to form a paste. Add this to the slow cooker, along with the cream, Parmesan and spinach. You may need to keep pushing the spinach leaves until they are submerged into the stock and start to wilt.

4 Drain the oil from the sundried tomatoes. Retain the oil (you can pop it back in the jar) as it is good to use as a flavoured oil in cooking. I store mine in the fridge. Add the tomatoes to the creamy chicken.

5 Season to taste.

6 Cook for a further 30 minutes on high.

7 Serve with steamed green vegetables.

NOTE

If you want to brown the chicken, you can do so before adding to the slow cooker. Simply heat some oil in a sauté pan and brown the chicken before placing into your slow cooker (if your slow cooker has a sauté facility you can use this instead of a separate pan). This step is purely for aesthetics only, so is not strictly necessary.

NUTRITIONAL INFORMATION PER SERVING

732 Kcals

40g fat

38g net carbohydrates

35g protein

INGREDIENTS

2–3 garlic cloves, crushed

1 small onion, finely chopped

100g smoked pancetta, diced

500g skinless, boneless chicken breast fillets

150ml white wine

250ml chicken stock

1 chicken gel stock cube

1 tbsp cornflour

50ml cold water

200ml double cream

50g Parmesan cheese, grated

75g baby leaf spinach

280g jar sundried tomatoes in oil, drained

seasoning, to taste

CREAMY CHICKEN & MUSHROOM PASTA

NUTRITIONAL INFORMATION PER SERVING

718 Kcals

36g fat

49g net carbohydrates

41g protein

INGREDIENTS

500g skinless, boneless chicken breast fillets, cut into strips or diced

1 onion, very finely chopped

200ml chicken stock

150ml white wine

300g Boursin garlic and herb cheese

250g pasta (I use tagliatelle or fettuccine)

100g chestnut mushrooms, halved or quartered

50g freshly grated Parmesan, to serve

You can't have a comfort cookbook without creamy pasta dishes. This feels a bit of a cheat recipe, to be honest, as you just chuck everything in, but it packs a punch and can be ready in as little as 2–3 hours if you wish. Remember, if your slow cooker tends to get a bit hot, it is always best to cook on low to avoid catching.

1 Preheat your slow cooker following the manufacturer's instructions.

2 Place the chicken, onion, stock and wine in the slow cooker. Place on high for 2 hours or low for 4–5 hours.

3 Forty-five minutes before serving, add the cheese, pasta and mushrooms. Combine well. Place the lid back on, turn to high (if not already on high) and cook for another 30–45 minutes until the pasta is cooked and the mushrooms soft.

4 Serve with a generous sprinkling of Parmesan.

ONE-POT CHICKEN STEW

SERVES 4

This is the perfect filling meal for the whole family and it's budget-friendly too. So easy, and so tasty. As with other recipes, you can, of course, use different vegetables, according to what you have in your fridge, but this is a basic staple, with family favourite peas and sweetcorn added at the last minute to maintain their colour and texture. This recipe uses standard potatoes, but when they are in season you can use new potatoes.

1 Preheat your slow cooker following the manufacturer's instructions.

2 Place all the ingredients into the slow cooker apart from the sweetcorn and peas. Season to taste.

3 Cook on low for 6–7 hours.

4 Thirty minutes before serving, add the defrosted peas and sweetcorn, stir well to combine, and turn the slow cooker to high.

5 Serve on its own with a garnish of fresh chopped rosemary.

NUTRITIONAL INFORMATION PER SERVING

345 Kcals

7.4g fat

33g net carbohydrates

33g protein

INGREDIENTS

2 garlic cloves, crushed

1 large onion, diced

1 pepper, roughly chopped

1–2 carrots, roughly chopped

1 stick celery, sliced

500g skinless, boneless chicken fillets (thigh or breast), roughly chopped

2–3 potatoes, peeled and roughly chopped

400g tin chopped tomatoes

300ml chicken stock

1 chicken stock gel cube

1 tsp dried thyme

½ tsp ground cumin

1 tsp sweet paprika

seasoning, to taste

75g frozen sweetcorn (defrosted)

75g frozen peas (defrosted)

fresh chopped rosemary, to garnish

3

Here are some of my family's favourite beef slow cooker recipes, which we enjoy regularly. The slow cooker is ideal for any cheaper cuts of meat that would otherwise be quite tough unless cooked long and slow. I have added some advice on cuts below, but always speak to your butcher to get advice on the best cuts of meat to suit your style of cooking.

BEST BEEF FOR SLOW COOKING

Most of the recipes in this chapter ask for stewing steak, which is the default terminology, but it is also known as braising steak, and can include skirt, flank or leg – think of the more muscly cuts of meat. In the US, braising steak is known as chuck or blade steak and, as our society becomes more Americanised, these terms are coming to be used more and more elsewhere too. You can also use brisket, which is a tad more fatty but still an excellent choice for slow cooking and a little more economical, but don't feel you have to stick to this; you can switch around and use other cuts, as detailed below.

Beef shin or leg is more lean muscle but benefits from a slow, low cook.

Beef cheeks are very flavoursome as well as being economical.

Oxtail needs a long cook but is bursting with great flavour.

Short ribs are becoming popular. They work well when cooked in a similar way to lamb shanks, in a rich sauce, but with the advantage of being a little cheaper than the lamb. ▶ ▶ ▶

Venison is meat from deer; it is darker than beef but has a great flavour. Most venison is not as gamey as it used to be, as it is no longer subjected to the traditional maturing process that increases the flavour. The meat's flavour also changes depending on what the animal eats: farmed corn-fed deer have a less gamey taste than do traditional wild deer. Venison is very nutrient-dense, but does not contain as much fat as beef and is high in protein. It is sometimes a little more expensive than beef, but if you see it on offer it is worth using.

You may notice that I have often added **liver or kidney** to the recipes. Some people don't like the thought of eating offal, however liver and kidney are so nutrient-dense, and so cheap to buy, it would be foolish for me not to include them.

MINCE

Mince does not always work well for long cooks. It can, however, be used in the slow cooker for a reduced time. You could ask your butcher to prepare some mince for you from a tougher cut of meat, which would work better for longer slow cooking, however I sometimes use beef shin or cheeks on a long and slow cook and then shred the meat into flakes once cooked – a little like when you prepare pulled pork. When I was growing up, we used to make our mince out of the remains of a cooked joint of beef, using a little hand-held mincer – a great idea to reduce waste.

BROWNING THE MEAT

All the recipes in this section give the option of sautéing the beef prior to slow cooking. Some people think this is a waste of time, however I find it not only helps to seal the meat but can also enhance the flavour, plus it stops the meat bleeding into the stock, which can give a curdled appearance. This is not essential so you can omit this step if you are the type of person who prefers to bung everything into the slow cooker at once. I use a multi-cooker so I simply switch from sauté to slow cooker function on my machine, which makes it much less of a faff. Some regular slow cookers have a sauté option too; if not, as described in the recipes, use your hob to start with, then transfer the meat to the slow cooker when it is sufficiently browned – which, I appreciate, is more time-consuming.

COMFORTING BEEF STEW WITH DUMPLINGS

SERVES 6

NUTRITIONAL INFORMATION PER SERVING

458 Kcals

14g fat

16g net carbohydrates

65g protein

INGREDIENTS

1–2 tbsp plain flour

2–3 tsp paprika

750g beef stewing steak, diced

olive oil or coconut oil

1 red onion, finely chopped

2 carrots, roughly chopped

2 parsnips, sliced

450ml beef or bone stock

1 bay leaf

1 rich beef gel stock cube

seasoning, to taste

FOR THE DUMPLINGS

100g self-raising flour

50g suet

2 tsp dried thyme (optional)

4 tbsp water

This is a traditional, old-fashioned beef stew, the type my dad would have absolutely adored. Thickly sliced carrots and parsnips accompany melt-in-the-mouth beef chunks in a rich gravy, making this casserole not only delicious but also economical. The dish is topped with fluffy dumplings for a filling, wholesome winter supper. If you like herby dumplings, just add dried thyme to the dumpling mixture (as described below).

1 Preheat your slow cooker following the manufacturer's instructions.

2 Place the flour in a bowl and mix in the paprika. Dip the beef chunks into this flour mix and ensure they are thoroughly coated.

3 If your slow cooker has a sauté option, you can use this; if not, use a sauté pan on the hob. Add the olive oil or coconut oil and heat. Add the beef and cook until brown, sealing in the flavour.

4 Place the meat in your slow cooker. Add all the remaining stew ingredients (not the dumpling mixture) and cook on low for 6–7 hours.

5 One hour before serving, make the dumpling dough by mixing the flour, suet and thyme (if using) together. Add the water a little at a time until it forms a nice dough, not too wet.

6 Work the dough into small balls and place these on top of the casserole. Place a tea towel under the lid of the slow cooker to absorb excess moisture. Place on high and cook for 1 hour until the dumplings fluff up. If you want to bake the dumplings instead, refer to the tip below.

7 Serve with steamed vegetables.

TOP TIP

If you like crispy dumplings rather than the doughy kind, you could cook them in the oven instead of with the casserole. Simply place the dumplings, once formed, in a greased muffin tin (one dumpling per muffin hole) and bake in the oven at 170°C for 15–20 minutes until golden and crisp.

BEEF BOURGUIGNON

SERVES 6

NUTRITIONAL INFORMATION PER SERVING

433 Kcals

20g fat

10g net carbohydrates

38g protein

INGREDIENTS

1–2 tbsp flour

750g beef braising steak, diced

olive oil or coconut oil

1 small red onion, diced

2 garlic cloves, roughly chopped

200g shallots, halved

200g thick pancetta, diced

1 carrot, diced

1 stick celery, diced

400g tin chopped tomatoes

400ml Burgundy red wine

1 tsp dried thyme

½ tsp rosemary

2 heaped tsp paprika

1 rich beef gel stock cube

seasoning, to taste

150g button mushrooms

This is perfect for dinner parties as you can prepare it in advance and enjoy being a host while it cooks, making it all look effortless! Remember you can get ahead by preparing this the day before as it really improves with age. When it's finished, I use the empty slow cooker to make my delicious Dauphinoise Potatoes (see page 147) and serve with some lovely steamed green veg.

1 Preheat your slow cooker following the manufacturer's instructions.

2 Place the flour in a bowl. Add the beef and ensure it is well coated with the flour.

3 Place some olive oil or coconut oil in the base of your sauté pan and add the beef (if your slow cooker has a sauté facility you can use this instead of a separate pan). Fry gently until it has browned. Place the beef in your slow cooker.

4 Add all the remaining ingredients apart from the mushrooms and combine well.

5 Cook on low for 8 hours.

6 Thirty minutes before serving, add the mushrooms, stirring well so they are submerged. Turn to high and cook for 30 minutes.

7 Serve with mashed potato or celeriac mash and steamed green leafy vegetables.

BEEF, LIVER & BACON CASSEROLE

It is nice to get back to some of the more traditional casseroles, from a time when we weren't afraid of using the most nutrient-dense foods, like liver, and combining them with a cheaper cut of beef to make a wholesome casserole. This is the ultimate comfort food when served with delicious buttery potato mash.

1 Preheat your slow cooker following the manufacturer's instructions.

2 Seal the meat by frying in a sauté pan with a little olive oil or coconut oil (if your slow cooker has a sauté facility you can use this instead of a separate pan).

3 Add all the remaining ingredients and combine well.

4 Cook on low for 6–8 hours until the beef and liver are very tender.

5 Serve with a creamy potato or celeriac mash and steamed green vegetables.

NUTRITIONAL INFORMATION PER SERVING

386 Kcals

13g fat

8.1g net carbohydrates

43g protein

INGREDIENTS

olive oil or coconut oil

500g stewing beef, diced

300g calf livers, diced

200g thick back bacon, thickly diced

2–3 garlic cloves, chopped

1 red onion, diced

400g tin chopped tomatoes

2 tbsp tomato purée

1 tsp dried thyme

1 bay leaf

1 tbsp Worcestershire sauce

450ml red wine

1 rich beef gel stock cube

seasoning, to taste

parsley leaves, to garnish

BEEF LASAGNE

NUTRITIONAL INFORMATION PER SERVING

553 Kcals

35g fat

25g net carbohydrates

32g protein

INGREDIENTS

1 tsp olive oil

1 large red onion, finely chopped

2–3 garlic cloves, finely chopped

1 red pepper, finely chopped

100g lardons or pancetta (optional)

500g beef mince

300ml beef or bone stock or red wine

400g tin chopped tomatoes

2 tbsp tomato purée

75g mushrooms, chopped

2 tsp dried oregano

1 tsp paprika

black pepper

300ml crème fraîche

100g mature cheese, grated (plus more to finish)

seasoning, to taste

6–8 no-precooking lasagne sheets

A real family favourite, made without too much fuss. You can batch cook the mince to use as a bolognese or a base for a chilli or lasagne and freeze it. If you are using this from frozen, ensure it is thoroughly defrosted. This recipe describes how to make this from scratch.

1 Preheat your slow cooker following the manufacturer's instructions.

2 Add the olive oil to a sauté pan. Add the onion and fry until soft and translucent (if your slow cooker has a sauté facility you can use this instead of a separate pan).

3 Add the garlic and pepper and cook for another couple of minutes.

4 Add the lardons (if using) and mince and cook until brown. Add the stock and cook for 2 more minutes.

5 Add the chopped tinned tomatoes and tomato purée. Stir well. Add the mushrooms and herbs and season with black pepper. Leave to simmer very gently for 5 minutes. If you are batch cooking, you can freeze what you don't want to use right away. If you have cooked this in your multi-cooker, remove it ready to form your lasagne.

6 Preheat your slow cooker on low.

7 Place the crème fraîche and grated cheese into a bowl and combine well. Season to taste and place to one side.

8 Place one-third of the mince mixture into the base of your slow cooker. Add lasagne sheets until the mince is covered. Top with a little of the crème fraîche mixture.

9 Continue to layer in this order, finishing with the crème fraîche mixture. Add more grated cheese and seasoning to finish.

10 Place a tea towel under the lid of the slow cooker. Cook on low for 5–6 hours.

11 Serve with a fresh green salad.

SPICY BEEF & BEAN GOULASH

SERVES 4

I love a goulash and this one has the added elements of red kidney beans and chunky mushrooms. It is the ultimate winter comfort food, with a kick of chilli and paprika, a flavour combination I absolutely adore. Mushrooms don't fare well in a slow cooker so need to be added in the last 30 minutes of cooking to retain their shape and flavour.

1 Preheat your slow cooker following the manufacturer's instructions.

2 Mix the flour and paprika together and season. Dip the beef chunks into the flour mix, ensuring they are evenly covered.

3 If you would like to brown the meat, you can do so on the hob, but if you have a multi-cooker, you can do this on the sauté setting. To brown the meat, place some olive oil in the pan, add the beef and cook for 5 minutes, turning regularly until it is sealed. This is not necessary however, so feel free to avoid this step.

4 Place all the ingredients in the slow cooker, apart from the mushrooms, and combine well.

5 Cover and cook on low for 6–8 hours.

6 Thirty minutes before serving, turn the slow cooker up to high and add the mushrooms, ensuring they are distributed evenly, ideally under the sauce of the dish to enable them to cook well.

7 Serve with steamed green vegetables and chunks of thick bread.

NUTRITIONAL INFORMATION PER SERVING

392 Kcals

8.5g fat

34g net carbohydrates

40g protein

INGREDIENTS

1–2 tbsp plain flour

1 heaped tsp smoked paprika

1 tsp sweet paprika

seasoning, to taste

500g stewing beef

olive oil (optional)

1 red onion, diced

2 garlic cloves, crushed

400g tin chopped tomatoes

2 carrots, sliced

400g tin red kidney beans

1–2 tsp chilli powder (depending on personal taste)

1 tbsp Worcestershire sauce

300ml beef or bone stock

1 rich beef gel stock cube

100g chestnut mushrooms, halved or quartered

2 bay leaves, to be removed before serving

MEXICAN BEEF, RICE & BEANS

NUTRITIONAL INFORMATION PER SERVING

639 Kcals

8.3g fat

90g net carbohydrates

45g protein

INGREDIENTS

500g minced beef

1 onion, diced

2 garlic cloves, crushed

2 chillies, deseeded and diced

1 red pepper, deseeded and diced

1 green pepper, deseeded and diced

2 tsp smoked paprika

½ tsp chilli flakes

1 tsp onion powder

1 tsp ground cumin

1 tsp dried oregano

1 rich beef gel stock cube

250ml beef stock

2 tbsp tomato purée

300g basmati rice, washed

400g tin red kidney beans (or black beans if you prefer)

200g tin sweetcorn, drained

This is the ultimate one-pot meal, delicious served with a dollop of guacamole and some sour cream and nachos. What could be better for a Saturday night with friends over? You can adjust the chillies to suit your own palate, but I like the flavour to have a bit of a kick.

1 Preheat your slow cooker following the manufacturer's instructions.

2 Place all the ingredients, apart from the rice, kidney beans and sweetcorn, into your slow cooker.

3 Cook on high for 2 hours.

4 After 2 hours, add the rice, kidney beans and sweetcorn, and continue to cook on high for another 30 minutes to 1 hour until the rice is cooked.

5 Serve with guacamole and sour cream, and tuck in with some nachos.

CHILLI CON CARNE

A lot of people fear cooking mince in the slow cooker, but if you buy good-quality lean mince and cook it for a shorter time, you will find it much more successful. This is the recipe for my traditional chilli con carne. I highly recommend batch cooking as it a real family favourite. My son loves this with rice but also on top of jacket potatoes, and has even been known to have it on hot dogs at a family BBQ!

1 Preheat your slow cooker following the manufacturer's instructions.

2 If your slow cooker has a sauté option, you can use this; if not, use your hob. Place the onion, star anise and garlic in a sauté pan and sauté for a couple of minutes. Add the beef and cook until brown, sealing in the meat and flavour. If you are using a higher-fat mince, you can drain off the fat at this stage if you wish. Remove the star anise.

3 Place into the slow cooker.

4 Add the warm stock, peppers, chillies, tinned tomatoes, tomato purée and remaining herbs and spices. Season to taste.

5 Cook on low for 2–3 hours.

6 Thirty minutes before serving, add the dark chocolate and red kidney beans. Turn onto high and cook for the remaining 30 minutes.

7 Serve with basmati rice or, for a low-calorie and low-carb option, serve with cauliflower rice, and with sour cream and lime wedges on the side.

NUTRITIONAL INFORMATION PER SERVING

458 Kcals

11g fat

30g net carbohydrates

53g protein

INGREDIENTS

1 large red onion, finely chopped

2 star anise

2 garlic cloves, crushed

750g lean beef mince

250ml bone or beef stock, warmed

2 red peppers, deseeded and sliced

1–2 chopped chillies (depending on desired flavour)

400g tin chopped tomatoes

3 tbsp tomato purée

1 tsp chilli powder

1 tsp ground cumin

1 heaped tsp smoked paprika

2 tsp paprika

1½ tsp dried marjoram

seasoning, to taste

1–2 squares 85% cocoa dark chocolate

400g tin red kidney beans, drained

lime wedges, to serve

PEPPERED ROAST BEEF

NUTRITIONAL INFORMATION
PER SERVING

269 Kcals

9.6g fat

3.9g net carbohydrates

41g protein

INGREDIENTS

1 large onion, cut into wedges

2 carrots, cut into thick batons

3 tbsp wholegrain mustard

1kg beef roasting joint

black pepper

500ml bone or beef stock

This makes a deliciously tender joint of beef. This way of cooking is also really useful when you want to free up space in your oven. Serve with roast potatoes, Yorkshire puddings and vegetables. Remember to retain the juices to use in your gravy!

1 Preheat your slow cooker following the manufacturer's instructions.

2 Place the onion and carrots into the base of the slow cooker.

3 Rub the mustard over the top of the beef joint and finish with a very generous layer of black pepper.

4 Place the meat on top of the bed of vegetables. Pour stock around the edges of the joint.

5 Cover and cook on low for 3–4 hours depending on how you like your beef.

6 Remove from the slow cooker and place on a carving board. Cover with foil and allow to rest for at least 15 minutes.

7 Drain the stock from the slow cooker and use some of it to make your gravy.

8 Serve with roast potatoes, Yorkshire puddings and a selection of vegetables.

TOP TIP

If you have more than one slow cooker, you could try out my delicious slow cooker roast potatoes (page 144), but for those who want to cook them in the oven, here are my top tips for the perfect roast potato. Peel the potatoes and cut them at an angle (keeping the pieces quite large). Boil the potatoes in water for 10 minutes. Place your roasting tray in the oven with your chosen fat (ideally goose fat, beef dripping or olive oil) at 190°C. When the potatoes have a soft edge to them, drain off the water and shake them gently in the pan to fluff them up. Remove the roasting tray from the oven and very gently add the potatoes, turning until they are completely covered in the oil. Sprinkle with paprika and semolina, then roast in a hot oven for 1½ hours until golden.

BEEF FAJITAS

This is perfect for stuffing in wraps or serving on a bed of rice. You can spice it up or down. I prefer it spicy as I love the kick. This does not need a long cook; you really don't want soggy peppers or overcooked beef.

1 Preheat your slow cooker following the manufacturer's instructions.

2 Place all the ingredients into your slow cooker and combine well. Season to taste.

3 Cook on high for 2–3 hours. The timing will depend on the thickness of the beef slices.

4 Once cooked, stir well. Use some tongs to lift out the beef mixture and place it into a serving dish. There will be some liquid left that you can discard.

5 Serve with tortilla wraps and tomato salsa.

NUTRITIONAL INFORMATION PER SERVING

250 Kcals

6.2g fat

15g net carbohydrates

30g protein

INGREDIENTS

500g lean beef, cut into strips

2 red onions, finely sliced

2 chillies, finely diced

1 tsp ground cumin

2 tsp paprika

1 tsp dried oregano

½ tsp allspice

3 tomatoes, finely diced

juice of 1 lime

1 red pepper, deseeded and sliced

1 yellow pepper, deseeded and sliced

1 green pepper, deseeded and sliced

seasoning, to taste

ASIAN BEEF

SERVES 4

NUTRITIONAL INFORMATION PER SERVING

353 Kcals

7.3g fat

25g net carbohydrates

46g protein

INGREDIENTS

4 tbsp dark soy sauce

4 tbsp hoisin sauce

3 garlic cloves, crushed

3cm piece fresh ginger, grated

2 tbsp brown sugar

1 onion, finely diced

750g stewing beef, sliced into thick strips

75ml water

1 tbsp cornflour (if needed)

6 spring onions, cut into 1cm diagonal slices, to serve

An Asian-inspired, flavoursome beef dish, delicious when served with rice. I prefer to make up the sauce and marinate the beef overnight or for a couple of hours before serving. I use large ziplock freezer bags for this process, but you can just place in a bowl and cover. Marinating enhances the flavour, but if you are in a hurry you can of course just add it all into the slow cooker.

1 Preheat your slow cooker following the manufacturer's instructions.

2 If you are marinating the beef, place all the ingredients, apart from the water, cornflour and spring onions, into the bag or dish, combine well and seal. Leave overnight or for at least 2 hours in the fridge.

3 When ready to cook, place all the ingredients into your slow cooker, including the water but not the cornflour or spring onions.

4 Cook on low for 4–5 hours. When ready to serve, check the consistency of the stock. If you want it thicker, you can mix cornflour with water to form a paste, add to the slow cooker, then turn to high and allow to cook for another 20–30 minutes until it has thickened.

5 When ready to serve, add the sliced spring onions and combine well before serving on a bed of rice.

TRADITIONAL MEATLOAF

This is a popular meal in the US, but it's so tasty that we ought to adopt it more elsewhere too! It works brilliantly in the slow cooker and also freezes well, so why not double up the recipe? I serve this with a delicious green salad in the warmer months, and with comforting steamed vegetables and mash in the winter months. It is very filling so you don't need very thick slices.

1 Preheat your slow cooker following the manufacturer's instructions.

2 Place the mince in a large bowl, add the remaining ingredients and combine well.

3 Transfer the meat mixture to your loaf tin. Alternatively, you can form it into a loaf shape with your hands. Place a rack on the base of your slow cooker (if you don't have a rack, roll up some tinfoil into long sausage shapes and place these on the base); this allows the fat to drain from the loaf. If you are opting for the free-form loaf and are worried about lifting it out without it breaking, you can also fold a long piece of foil lengthways, to form a wide strap. Place this on the rack (or foil base) before you place the loaf onto it, leaving enough strap sticking out either side of the loaf to enable you to lift it out when cooked.

4 Mix together the sauce ingredients and coat the top of the loaf with the mixture. You can leave some of the sauce if you prefer to coat when serving (or double up the quantities if you need more).

5 Cook on low for 5–6 hours.

6 Remove the loaf carefully from the slow cooker – it can be quite fragile, so handle with care.

7 Serve either hot or cold.

NUTRITIONAL INFORMATION PER SERVING

435 Kcals

30g fat

6g net carbohydrates

33g protein

INGREDIENTS

750g minced beef

150g finely chopped back bacon, lardons or pancetta

50g breadcrumbs

1 onion, finely chopped

2 garlic cloves, crushed

2 tsp dried oregano

1 tsp paprika

1 tsp dried thyme

1 tbsp yeast extract

seasoning, to taste

1 egg, beaten

2 tbsp tomato purée

1 tbsp Worcestershire sauce

FOR THE RED SAUCE

2 tbsp tomato purée

2 tbsp brown sauce

1 tsp white wine vinegar

2 tbsp brown sugar

1 tsp onion powder

seasoning, to taste

4

This chapter contains recipes using pork, ham/gammon, sausages and bacon. They all work well in the slow cooker. Pork has the added advantage of being an economical and surprisingly healthy meat, high in protein, iron and B vitamins.

Pork is often cheaper to buy than chicken, especially if you are using something like pork loin or pork chops. You can buy lots of different cuts that work well in the slow cooker. I use pork belly, pork tenderloins, pork cheek and pork shoulder. Speak to your butcher for cost-cutting suggestions that work well when slow cooked.

SAUSAGES AND BACON

The slow cooker does not brown meat and if you are cooking something like sausages they do need some colour, so I would advise you to either cook them completely and add them in the last stages of the slow cook, or to brown them before adding them to the slow cooker. Both methods work well. I strongly advise against placing them into the slow cooker raw as you will not only end up with a very unappetising sausage, but also one that has lost its shape and texture during the longer cook.

Bacon can be added to the slow cooker in its raw state; it will still give flavour but can remain flesh-coloured, so if you want a nice colour as well as a crispy texture to your bacon, you will have to brown/crisp it first.

BACON-WRAPPED PORK TENDERLOIN WITH CREAMY MUSTARD SAUCE

SERVES 8

NUTRITIONAL INFORMATION PER SERVING

717 Kcals

58g fat

3.5g net carbohydrates

42g protein

INGREDIENTS

1 tsp olive oil

2 tsp dried thyme

2 tsp dried rosemary

2 tsp Dijon mustard

3 garlic cloves, chopped

1.5kg pork loin joint

seasoning, to taste

200g streaky bacon

1 large onion, sliced

350ml bone, pork or chicken stock

1–2 tsp cornflour (optional)

FOR THE MUSTARD SAUCE

250ml double cream

1 tbsp wholegrain mustard

1 tsp Dijon mustard

25ml (1 shot) brandy

seasoning, to taste

1–2 tbsp milk (optional)

Pork tenderloin works brilliantly in the slow cooker. In this recipe, the pork is wrapped in bacon – delicious served with green vegetables, mash and a creamy mustard sauce.

1 Preheat your slow cooker following the manufacturer's instructions.

2 Mix together the oil, thyme, rosemary, mustard and garlic. Spread this mixture over the pork loin. Season to taste before wrapping well with the streaky bacon, ensuring there are no gaps.

3 Place the onion on the base of the slow cooker and add the stock, before gently placing the pork loin so it sits well on the base of onions.

4 Cook on low for 6 hours.

5 When cooked, remove the pork from the slow cooker and wrap it in foil to rest. You can then drain out the stock and use this as a gravy if you wish. If you need to thicken it, pour into a pan and heat gently until it starts to thicken and reduce. You can add 1–2 tsp of cornflour, mixed with water, if you need to thicken it more.

6 To make the mustard sauce, place the cream and mustard into a pan then add the brandy. Heat gently while stirring continually. Add salt and pepper to taste. Stir until combined and creamy. If the sauce feels too thick, slowly add milk until you get the consistency you desire.

7 Serve with mash and steamed vegetables.

HAM, MAC & CHEESE

SERVES 4–6

You can't really have a comfort recipe book without some form of mac & cheese. This one has chunks of ham in it, perfect to use up any leftovers from a gammon joint – or, for a cheap and easy alternative to a gammon joint, use ham hock or bacon hock. You get so much more for your money. See page 96 for my Cider-Infused Gammon Joint recipe.

1 Preheat your slow cooker following the manufacturer's instructions.

2 Add all the ingredients into the slow cooker and combine.

3 Season to taste.

4 Cook on low for 2 hours, or until the pasta is cooked.

5 If you want a golden baked top, once cooked, you can pour the mixture into a baking dish, sprinkle with some additional cheese and place under the grill for 3 minutes until golden.

NUTRITIONAL INFORMATION PER SERVING

615 Kcals

32g fat

43g net carbohydrates

39g protein

INGREDIENTS

1 litre milk

250g mature Cheddar cheese, grated

125g cream cheese

40g Parmesan cheese

1–2 tbsp nutritional yeast flakes (optional)

½ tsp English mustard powder (optional)

300g dried macaroni

300g cooked gammon, diced

seasoning, to taste

BRAISED CHEEKS IN RED WINE & THYME SAUCE

SERVES 6

NUTRITIONAL INFORMATION
PER SERVING

398 Kcals

27g fat

7.5g net carbohydrates

29g protein

INGREDIENTS

700g pig cheeks (cut in half
if large)

200g chorizo, diced

1 red onion, diced

2 garlic cloves, crushed

1–2 chillies, deseeded and finely
chopped

1 red pepper, deseeded and diced

2 tsp smoked paprika

1 tsp dried parsley

2 tsp dried thyme

½ tsp dried marjoram

400g tin chopped tomatoes

1 tbsp tomato purée

350ml red wine

2 rich beef gel stock cubes

seasoning, to taste

If you have never had pig cheeks, I urge you to try them. Beef or ox cheeks can also be used in this recipe, and you can get them all from your butcher. Cheeks work brilliantly in the slow cooker as they benefit from a long, slow cook. This dish is delicious served with steamed savoy cabbage and mash with a drizzle of sour cream.

1 Preheat your slow cooker following the manufacturer's instructions.

2 Place all the ingredients into the slow cooker and combine well. Season to taste.

3 Cook on low for 7–8 hours.

4 Serve with steamed green vegetables and mash.

ULTIMATE SAUSAGE & MASH

SERVES 4

This is a bit of a cheat meal, to be honest. I was brought up to always fill an oven when it is on and plan my cooking for the week. As I mentioned in the introduction to this section, sausages don't look great when slow cooked, so I tend to brown them first or cook them in advance (often the day before) and use the slow cooker to create a thick mushroom and onion gravy for them to be immersed in. This is the ultimate sausage and mash combo – perfect after a busy day.

1 Preheat your slow cooker following the manufacturer's instructions.

2 Add the onions to the slow cooker, with the bay leaf, thyme, tomato purée, beef stock and red wine.

3 Cook on high for 2 hours.

4 After 2 hours and with another hour to go until serving, mix the cornflour with water and combine well. Pour into the slow cooker. Add the mushrooms and sausages.

5 Thirty minutes before serving, steam your potatoes until soft.

6 Mash the potatoes with butter and wholegrain mustard. Season to taste.

7 Serve the sausage and mash with steamed vegetables.

NOTE

My sausages have been cooked in the oven the day before and are stored in the fridge ready to use.

NUTRITIONAL INFORMATION PER SERVING

583 Kcals

32g fat

38g net carbohydrates

18g protein

INGREDIENTS

2 red onions, sliced

1 bay leaf

1 tsp dried thyme

1 tbsp tomato purée

1 rich beef gel stock cube

300ml red wine

1–3 tsp cornflour (depending on desired thickness)

a little water

125g chestnut mushrooms, thickly sliced

8 good-quality sausages (I use high meat content, gluten-free), pre-cooked

FOR THE MASH POTATO

500g floury potatoes, peeled and diced

50g butter

1 tsp wholegrain mustard (optional)

seasoning, to taste

CIDER-INFUSED GAMMON JOINT

SERVES 6–8

NUTRITIONAL INFORMATION
PER SERVING

137 Kcals

7.5g fat

3.1g net carbohydrates

13g protein

INGREDIENTS

2 onions, thickly sliced

1.5kg gammon joint

2 bay leaves

1 tbsp black peppercorns

450ml dry cider

FOR THE COATING
(IF ROASTING)

1 tbsp butter

2 tbsp runny honey

1 tbsp brown sugar

1 tbsp Dijon mustard

I love slow-cooked gammon and there are a variety of ways you can cook it. Sometimes I do it in just water, finishing with a roast in the oven to crisp up the edges. This recipe harnesses the sweetness of cider to make a delicious flavour.

1 Preheat your slow cooker following the manufacturer's instructions.

2 Put the onions on the base of the slow cooker. Place the gammon joint on top of the onions. Add the bay leaves and peppercorns.

3 Pour in the cider.

4 Cook on low for 6–8 hours or on high for 4 hours.

5 When cooked, discard the onions and juice.

ROASTING

1 You can roast the gammon after slow cooking if you want to crisp up the fat on the outside. Remove it from the slow cooker and score with a sharp knife to form diamonds. If you want to be a bit fancy, you can stud the fat with cloves. Place the gammon joint on a rack in a roasting tray.

2 Put the butter, honey, brown sugar and Dijon mustard in a saucepan and heat very gently until they are all combined. Brush this mixture onto your gammon joint.

3 Place in a preheated oven at 190°C and cook for 30 minutes until golden.

4 Remove from the oven and allow to rest before slicing.

TOP TIP

If you do not want to cook in the oven, you can remove all the fat from the gammon before placing it into the slow cooker. Leave the fat on if you will be crisping in the oven, as this also protects the joint from drying out.

POTATO, CHEESE & BACON LAYER

SERVES 4

A supremely comforting supper that is also nice served cold with salad for a great picnic lunch. My son also loves this with lashings of baked beans. This recipe uses garlic, onion and bacon, but you can fill with layers of your choice or opt for different cheese or herbs to create new flavours. It is a very versatile recipe.

1 Line your slow cooker with baking parchment, slow cooker liner or a cake liner. If you prefer, you can grease it well with butter, but if your slow cooker has a tendency to catch in places, I urge you to line it.

2 Preheat your slow cooker following the manufacturer's instructions.

3 Once you have all the ingredients prepared, it is simply a matter of layering. I start with the potato, add some onion and garlic, bacon and then cheese, and continue layering in this order until all the main ingredients have been used.

4 Mix the eggs with the double cream, add the herbs and the Parmesan to the mixture, and pour this over the layers.

5 Place a tea towel under the lid of the slow cooker to help absorb any moisture. Cook on high for 2½ hours. If your slow cooker is a little on the hot side, opt to cook on low for 5–6 hours instead, or until the potatoes are cooked through.

6 Serve with baked beans or salad.

NUTRITIONAL INFORMATION PER SERVING

757 Kcals

55g fat

33g net carbohydrates

30g protein

INGREDIENTS

3 potatoes, peeled and thinly sliced

1 large onion, thinly sliced

2 garlic cloves, crushed

6 rashers thick back bacon, diced

200g mature Cheddar cheese

6 large eggs, beaten

200ml double cream

1 tsp oregano or mixed Italian herbs

50g grated Parmesan cheese

5

Lamb

Lamb works brilliantly in the slow cooker, benefiting from the long, slow cook. You can buy leg, breast, loin and neck of lamb, shoulder, saddle or rump. As with any meat, speak to your butcher about the best cuts of lamb for your chosen dish.

The term lamb applies only to a young lamb. Although lamb is readily available all year round, you will notice differences in flavour depending on when you buy: spring lamb is a tender meat but lacks the flavour of autumn lamb. After the animal is around two years old the meat is known as mutton. It has a stronger flavour than lamb, almost gamey in taste, and works really well in the slow cooker. I have used the name lamb in these recipes, but you can also use mutton. Mutton works particularly well in curries.

You can buy diced lamb in the supermarket, which is suitable for the slow cooker. You can also use diced lamb for most of the casserole, ragout, curry or tagine dishes. If you speak to your butcher, they can be more specific about the cheaper cuts. For example, the scrag and middle neck is ideal for slow cooking and an inexpensive cut. You can also use shoulder, which is cheaper than leg of lamb. Lamb shanks are amazing when cooked in the slow cooker, but they are not the cheapest cut, which is why, with the exception of the first recipe in this chapter, I have not included them here. However, if you like lamb shanks, you will probably love oxtail or beef short ribs cooked the same way.

LAMB SHANKS

SERVES 4

NUTRITIONAL INFORMATION
PER SERVING

454 Kcals

23.4g fat

18.8g net carbohydrates

38g protein

INGREDIENTS

2 red onions, finely sliced

3 garlic cloves, crushed

2 sticks celery, finely sliced

1 leek, finely sliced

2 carrots, finely diced

4 lamb shanks

400g tin chopped tomatoes

2 tsp tomato purée

1 tbsp balsamic vinegar

200ml red wine

200ml bone, lamb or vegetable stock

1 tsp paprika

1–2 tsp mint sauce

2 bay leaves

sprigs of fresh thyme and rosemary

2–3 tsp cornflour (optional)

a little water (optional)

seasoning, to taste

I have included this in a couple of my other slow cooker books, but as it's a great family classic and so comforting when served with a lovely creamy mash, it would seem wrong not to include it here too! Lamb shanks are more expensive in the supermarket, so speak to your butcher to get the best deal. Remember, lamb can also be cheaper at certain times of the year – usually spring – if you're buying local.

1 Preheat your slow cooker following the manufacturer's instructions.

2 Prepare all the vegetables, making sure all the pieces are roughly the same size, so they cook evenly.

3 Place all the ingredients in the slow cooker. Make sure they are combined well and evenly distributed.

4 Cook on low for 8–10 hours until the lamb is tender.

5 Prior to serving, if your liquid is too thin, stir in 2–3 teaspoons of cornflour dissolved in a little water, then turn up the heat for 5–10 minutes to thicken.

6 Season to taste before serving.

DONER KEBAB

This is very easy to make and much healthier than the takeaway alternative. Serve with some salad, in between some pitta or flatbreads. I've used lamb mince here, but you can also use beef, chicken or turkey mince for a variation on this recipe.

1 Preheat your slow cooker following the manufacturer's instructions.

2 Place all the ingredients into your food processor and whizz until smooth.

3 Oil a square of foil.

4 Tip out the meat mixture and form it into a thick sausage shape. Place this onto your foil and wrap tightly.

5 Place the foiled meat into your slow cooker and cook on low for 5–6 hours.

6 When ready to serve, unwrap the foil, remove the meat and place on a chopping board. Thinly slice your kebab meat and serve with salad stuffed into pitta or flatbreads.

NUTRITIONAL INFORMATION PER SERVING

413 Kcals

27g fat

2.9g net carbohydrates

39g protein

INGREDIENTS

750g lamb mince

½ onion, finely chopped

3 garlic cloves, crushed

2 tsp chilli powder (or to taste)

1 tsp ground cumin

1 tsp ground coriander

2 tsp dried oregano

2 tsp smoked paprika

seasoning, to taste

1 egg, beaten

LAMB SHOULDER

SERVES 6

NUTRITIONAL INFORMATION
PER SERVING

510 Kcals

37g fat

3.1g net carbohydrates

36g protein

INGREDIENTS

1 large onion, sliced

1 large carrot, sliced

200ml bone or lamb stock

100ml red wine

1.5kg lamb shoulder

3–4 garlic cloves, thickly sliced

2–3 sprigs fresh rosemary (optional)

seasoning, to taste

I love cooking this in my slow cooker. It is so tender and tasty, with very little fuss. Serve with roast potatoes (page 144) and vegetables for the perfect Sunday roast.

1 Preheat your slow cooker following the manufacturer's instructions.

2 Place the sliced onion and carrot in the base of your slow cooker.

3 Combine the stock and wine and pour over the onion and carrots.

4 Using a very sharp knife, cut small holes in the top of the lamb shoulder, just enough to push in some of the thickly sliced garlic slivers. You can also add some sprigs of rosemary if you wish.

5 Season well with salt and pepper.

6 Place the lamb shoulder into the slow cooker, on the bed of onion and carrots.

7 Cook on low for 5–7 hours, or until tender (the timing will depend on the size of the lamb shoulder).

8 Once cooked, remove from the slow cooker and allow to sit, covered, for 20–30 minutes before carving. Retain the stock for your gravy.

9 Serve with roast potatoes and steamed vegetables.

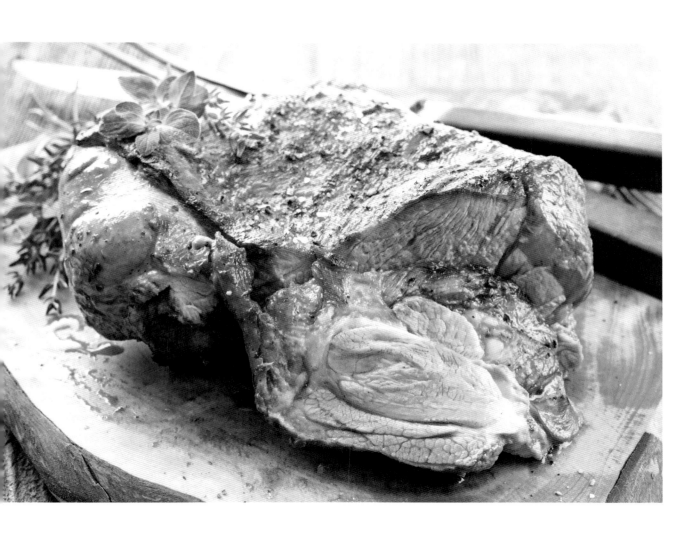

KASMIRI LAMB

SERVES 6

This wonderful lamb curry has an incredible depth of flavour. If you have never made a curry from scratch, don't be daunted – once you have a cupboard stocked with good spices, it will revolutionise your cooking. It is well worth investing in a variety of quality spices and using fresh ingredients – you will never want to use a jar of curry sauce again! Always cook this on low as the spices infuse with the lamb so much better when cooked low and slow.

1 Preheat your slow cooker following the manufacturer's instructions.

2 To make the curry paste, place all the ingredients into your food processor and pulse until smooth and combined. Season to taste.

3 Place this and the remaining ingredients into the slow cooker. Combine well.

4 Cook on low for 8–10 hours for a very tender lamb.

5 When ready to serve, garnish with sliced red chillies and coriander leaves.

6 Serve on a bed of rice. To reduce the carbs, why not serve with cauliflower rice instead?

TOP TIP

This recipe makes enough curry for six people. Freeze any remaining curry in small portions. I like to build up a collection of different curries ready for a 'fakeaway' evening. You can also double or triple the amount of curry paste and freeze it in portions.

NUTRITIONAL INFORMATION
PER SERVING

408 Kcals

24g fat

11g net carbohydrates

34g protein

INGREDIENTS
FOR THE CURRY PASTE

2cm piece fresh ginger, finely chopped

1 chilli, finely chopped

1 tsp ground cumin

2 tsp ground cardamom (or crush 6 green cardamom seeds)

1 tsp ground coriander

3 garlic cloves, finely chopped

1 tbsp Kashmiri garam masala

1 tsp ground turmeric

2 bay leaves

2 tbsp tomato purée

3 tomatoes, chopped

seasoning, to taste

750g lamb, diced

2 onions, sliced

1 green pepper, deseeded and diced

100g ground almonds

250g natural full-fat Greek yoghurt

sliced red chillies and coriander leaves, to garnish

MEDITERRANEAN LAMB

SERVES 4

NUTRITIONAL INFORMATION
PER SERVING

517 Kcals

30g fat

18g net carbohydrates

33g protein

INGREDIENTS

500g lamb, diced

1 onion, diced

3 garlic cloves, crushed

2 red peppers, deseeded
and sliced

150ml red wine

400g tin chopped tomatoes

3 tbsp sundried tomato paste

2 tsp dried thyme

2 tsp marjoram

1 aubergine, diced

parsley, to garnish

100g feta cheese (optional),
to serve

This tasty lamb dish comes in a rich tomato sauce. It works brilliantly when combined with the contrast of feta cheese to make a wholesome summer casserole, and is even more delicious when served with crusty bread and a handful of Kalamata olives added just prior to serving.

1 Preheat your slow cooker following the manufacturer's instructions.

2 Add all the ingredients apart from the aubergine, parsley and feta.

3 Cook on low for 6 hours.

4 Two hours before serving, add the aubergine. Turn back to low and cook for another 1½–2 hours.

5 When ready to serve, garnish with parsley. It is also delicious when served with feta cheese crumbled on top.

CHORBA FRIK

SERVES 4

This is a traditional soup/stew served in Algeria, Tunisia and Libya. I have popped it into the lamb chapter instead of the soup chapter as to me it is more of a meal and very filling when served with bread. Just like all lamb dishes, this really benefits from a long, slow cook.

1 Preheat your slow cooker following the manufacturer's instructions.

2 Add all the ingredients apart from the chickpeas and freekeh. Cook on low for 8 hours.

3 One hour before serving, add the chickpeas and freekeh. Turn up to high and cook for the remaining hour.

4 Garnish with coriander leaves. Serve with bread.

NUTRITIONAL INFORMATION
PER SERVING

400 Kcals

14g fat

28g net carbohydrates

36g protein

INGREDIENTS

500g lamb, diced

1 large onion, diced

2 red chillies, deseeded and diced

2 garlic cloves, crushed

1 stick celery, diced

400g tin chopped tomatoes

2 tsp ras el hanout

1 tsp ground cinnamon

1 tsp chilli powder

1 tsp asafoetida

2 tsp ground coriander

2 tsp dried mint

2 tbsp tomato purée

seasoning, to taste

400g tin chickpeas

100g freekeh (you can use barley, quinoa or bulgur wheat if you prefer)

coriander leaves, to garnish

6

Fish is normally cooked fast, so some may question why we would want to use a slow cooker. You may be surprised at what you can do with it, though, and how the fish can taste when cooked this way. The slow cooker also traps the odours, so your kitchen doesn't smell too fishy. Below are some tips for cooking fish in your slow cooker – you may want to adapt your own recipes to suit or try something new using this advice. Speak to your fishmonger to discuss the right type of fish for the slow cooker.

GENERAL COOKING

Cooking fish in the slow cooker can really enhance its flavour, however you will have to consider cooking times. We are used to slow cookers fitting around our busy lives, but fish recipes might not be so accommodating. Fish does not need long cooking times, so you will be looking at a maximum of 3–4 hours and it needs to be eaten straight away as it will dry out if left on warm. This may make fish a less viable option if you want to prepare your slow cooker to cook all day when you are at work.

POACHING

Poaching fish takes only about 45 minutes on high. Add your fish with the stock or water and simply poach with a few herbs to add flavour.

SHELLFISH

If you like shellfish, such as prawns, crabs, lobster and so on, add them towards the end of the cooking time otherwise they may spoil. If cooking on high, this can be in the last 20 minutes. If you are using frozen, make sure they are defrosted completely before adding to the stock pot.

SPICY PRAWN, CHICKEN & CHORIZO PAELLA

SERVES 4–6

NUTRITIONAL INFORMATION
PER SERVING

351 Kcals

13g fat

24g net carbohydrates

30g protein

INGREDIENTS

2 tsp chilli oil

1 onion, finely chopped

3 garlic cloves, crushed

2 red chillies, finely chopped

1 red pepper, deseeded and diced

125g chorizo, diced

300g skinless, boneless chicken
fillet (breast or thigh), diced

1 tbsp smoked paprika

1 tsp dried parsley

125ml white wine

750ml hot chicken, fish or
vegetable stock

300g paella rice

400g tin cherry tomatoes
(use standard chopped tomatoes
if preferred)

100g frozen peas, defrosted

300g peeled king prawns

lemon wedges, to serve

This is a different take on the traditional paella, with chorizo, prawn and chicken served with the traditional paella flavours. It is a quick and easy meal, ready in just over 2 hours. As with all fish meals made in the slow cooker, it takes very little time for the prawns to cook, so these are added late on.

1 Preheat your slow cooker following the manufacturer's instructions.

2 If you have a sauté facility in your slow cooker you can use this, otherwise add the oil to a sauté pan, add the onion, garlic, chilli, pepper, chorizo and chicken, and cook for 5–8 minutes until starting to soften.

3 Transfer to the slow cooker and turn to high. Add the paprika, parsley, wine and stock and combine well.

4 Add the rice and cherry tomatoes and cook for 1½–2 hours.

5 Add the peas and prawns and cook for another 20–30 minutes, or until the rice is cooked to your taste.

6 Serve with a wedge of lemon.

CAJUN FISH GUMBO

SERVES 4

A tasty fish stew, with a rich, slightly spicy stock. I have opted for a very simple fish selection here, but you can add whatever fish fillets or seafood you prefer. Speak to your fishmonger for recommendations. For the nutritional analysis I have used salmon.

1 Preheat your slow cooker following the manufacturer's instructions.

2 In a sauté pan (or use the sauté facility in your slow cooker if it has one) add the olive oil and the onion, peppers, celery, carrots, garlic and chorizo. Cook for 5–8 minutes until softened.

3 Transfer to the slow cooker (if you've sautéed separately) along with the chopped tomatoes, tomato paste, herbs and spices, and white wine.

4 Add the fish fillets.

5 Cook on high for 2–3 hours or on low for 3–5 hours (timings depend on the thickness and size of your fish fillets).

6 Thirty minutes before the end of the cooking time, add the prawns, fresh parsley and coriander, and turn to high for the last half hour.

7 Serve with a few spoonsful of cooked basmati rice stirred into the casserole.

8 Finish with a garnish of fresh coriander leaves.

TOP TIP

This is delicious served with cooked brown rice added to the stew just before serving.

NUTRITIONAL INFORMATION PER SERVING

740 Kcals

43g fat

16g net carbohydrates

59g protein

INGREDIENTS

2 tsp olive oil (if sautéing separately)

1 large onion, finely chopped

2 red peppers, deseeded and finely chopped

1 stick celery, finely diced

1 large carrot, finely diced

3 garlic cloves, crushed

250g chorizo, sliced or diced

400g tin chopped tomatoes

2 tsp sundried tomato paste

1 tsp dried parsley

1 tsp smoked paprika

2 tsp Cajun spice mix

200ml white wine

500g fish fillets, diced (you can use any white fish, salmon or fish pie mix)

350g prawns, peeled and deveined

small handful fresh parsley leaves

small handful fresh coriander leaves (plus a little extra to garnish)

MEDITERRANEAN FISH PARCEL

SERVES 4

NUTRITIONAL INFORMATION PER SERVING

175 Kcals

7.7g fat

2.4g net carbohydrates

23g protein

INGREDIENTS

2 garlic cloves, crushed

1 fennel bulb, cut into quarters

8–12 fresh olives of your choice

8–12 cherry tomatoes

1 tbsp capers (optional)

2 sprigs thyme

4–6 basil leaves

4 cod fillets (approx. 500g)

2–3 lemon slices

seasoning, to taste

2 tbsp olive oil

Such a simple dish, but it tastes wonderful. For ease (and for the nutritional analysis), I have used thick cod fillets in this recipe, but you can use any fish you wish – it works brilliantly with salmon. I use parchment to create my parcel/bag, but you can use foil if you prefer. I just think the parchment looks a bit nicer when serving. If you like to have the strength of foil, I highly recommend using parchment-lined foil.

1 Preheat your slow cooker following the manufacturer's instructions.

2 Place one 30cm square of parchment on your worktop, or you can make smaller individual parcels if you prefer.

3 Place the garlic, fennel, olives, cherry tomatoes, capers (if using), thyme and basil into the centre of the parchment. Add the cod fillets and top with slices of lemon.

4 Season thoroughly before adding a small drizzle of olive oil (roughly 1–2 teaspoons per fish fillet).

5 Wrap the foil securely and place the parcel in the base of the slow cooker.

6 Replace the lid and cook on low for 2–3 hours (the timing depends on the size and thickness of your fillets).

7 Be careful when removing the parcel(s) from the slow cooker as they can be quite fragile.

8 Serve with a variety of salads.

COMFORTING FISH PIE

SERVES 6

Fish pie is the ultimate comfort food, so I really had to include it in this book. The creamy sauce combines well with the cheesy mash. This is a two-step process as you cook the base in the slow cooker before adding the cheesy mash, but don't let that put you off – it is a really tasty dish.

1 Preheat your slow cooker following the manufacturer's instructions.

2 Place the fish in the base of your slow cooker dish. Cover the fish with the onion and season to taste.

3 Mix the cornflour in a jug with 3 tablespoons water until dissolved.

4 Combine the cornflour mixture with the cream, cheese, mustard and parsley, and pour this over the fish.

5 Cook on low for 1 hour.

6 Meanwhile you can prepare the mash topping. Cut your peeled potatoes into thick chunks and steam until they are soft. When soft, mash with the butter. Season to taste before adding the grated cheese. Combine well.

7 When the hour is up, add the prawns, sweetcorn and peas (if using) to your slow cooker, and combine well.

8 Place the mash on top of the fish base and smooth it with a fork. If you want to be a bit fancy, you can pipe it on.

9 Place a tea towel under the lid. Change the setting to high and cook for another 30 minutes to 1 hour.

10 Before serving, if you want a golden topping, remove the dish from the slow cooker, add more grated cheese and place it under the grill until golden.

11 Serve with steamed green vegetables.

TOP TIP

Try a variation on the mash – mix some cauliflower and broccoli to make a tasty topping that is lower in carbohydrates. Alternatively, you can opt for a celeriac mash.

NUTRITIONAL INFORMATION PER SERVING

861 Kcals

64g fat

39g net carbohydrates

31g protein

INGREDIENTS

350g selection of fish pieces (or fish pie mix)

1 small onion, diced

seasoning, to taste

1 tbsp cornflour

3 tbsp water

500ml double cream

100g Cheddar cheese, grated

½ tsp mustard powder (or 1 tsp Dijon mustard)

small handful fresh parsley

200g prawns, peeled and deveined

75g sweetcorn (optional)

75g peas (optional)

FOR THE TOPPING

1kg potatoes, peeled and diced

50g butter

100g mature Cheddar cheese, grated

BRAZILIAN-STYLE FISH STEW

NUTRITIONAL INFORMATION
PER SERVING

287 Kcals

14g fat

8.8g net carbohydrates

30g protein

INGREDIENTS

2–3 garlic cloves, crushed

1 onion, diced

1 red pepper, deseeded and diced

250ml coconut cream

400g tin chopped tomatoes

2 tbsp tomato purée

1 tsp cayenne pepper

2 tsp paprika

2 tsp freeze-dried coriander

1 tsp marjoram

juice of 1 lime

seasoning, to taste

500g white fish fillets

This is traditionally known as *moqueca baiana*, which basically is a lovely fish stew in a creamy tomato base, but I have adapted it to suit my personal taste. I do hope you enjoy it. For this recipe I have used white fish fillets such as cod, pollock, hake or haddock, but you can, of course, use salmon if you prefer, or even a mixture.

1 Preheat your slow cooker following the manufacturer's instructions.

2 Place all the ingredients apart from the fish fillets into the slow cooker and combine well. Season to taste.

3 Cook on high for 1 hour.

4 After an hour, add the fish fillets. You can leave these whole or dice them – whatever you prefer. Continue to cook on high for another 1–2 hours until the fish is cooked (timings depend on the size of the fish fillets).

5 Serve with hunks of thick bread.

7

This chapter contains recipes that are suitable for vegans and vegetarians, but don't think they are not useful if you eat meat. These recipes are all delicious and suitable for meat-eaters too! Family favourites packed with flavour.

Vegan and plant-based lifestyles are becoming increasingly popular. Some people have adopted this way of eating 100 per cent, while others try to have one or two days a week when they eat vegan or vegetarian. I would encourage everyone who is thinking about veganism to opt for a real food diet and avoid 'fake/faux' manufactured products, which are highly processed and very inflammatory due to the high levels of oils used. It is so important to ensure you have enough quality nutrients in your diet – in particular, good protein from a variety of foods, healthy fats, minerals and vitamins. You will find it harder to get a complete protein profile, good-quality omega-3, iron and vitamin B12, making it even more vital to get your food from natural sources that are nutrient-rich. For more information, you could check out one of my other books, *The Part-Time Vegan*.

If you are vegetarian, there are curds you can use as a protein source, such as paneer (which is a curd made from cow's milk), tofu or tempeh. You can also include beans and pulses, which are cheap but nutritious and help to bulk out meals. Nuts and seeds, including nut butters, are also very nutritious options.

The slow cooker works well with both vegan and vegetarian dishes. I have included a selection of my personal favourites here.

MEXICAN SPICED BEAN POT

SERVES 4

This is a delicious dish for plant-based days, and has the benefit of being very high in protein and fibre. You can enjoy this as a winter warmer as well as in the summer months due to its delicious flavours. I find it also makes a great lunch. Garnish with diced avocado, and serve with lime wedges, guacamole and nachos.

1 Preheat your slow cooker following the manufacturer's instructions.

2 Place all the ingredients into the slow cooker, apart from the sweetcorn, avocado and extra chilli for garnish.

3 Cook on low for 7–8 hours. You can also cook this on high for 3–4 hours if you prefer a quicker meal.

4 Thirty minutes before serving, add the sweetcorn, then turn up to high to cook for the last half hour.

5 Finish with a garnish of avocado and chilli.

6 Serve with guacamole and nachos.

NUTRITIONAL INFORMATION PER SERVING

497 Kcals

19g fat

52g net carbohydrates

20g protein

INGREDIENTS

3 garlic cloves, crushed

1 large red onion, finely chopped

2 red chillies, deseeded and finely chopped

2 red peppers, deseeded and thickly diced

1 stick celery, diced

1 large carrot, diced

400g tin chopped tomatoes

3 tbsp sundried tomato paste

2 x 400g tins mixed beans, drained

250–350ml vegetable stock

3 tsp dried oregano

1 tsp rosemary

1 tsp chilli powder

1 tsp ground cumin

2 tsp paprika

1 tsp parsley

seasoning, to taste

150g sweetcorn

1 avocado, diced

1 chilli, thickly sliced, to garnish

VEGETABLE, BEAN & QUINOA CASSEROLE

SERVES 4

NUTRITIONAL INFORMATION PER SERVING

476 Kcals

13g fat

61g net carbohydrates

20g protein

INGREDIENTS

3 garlic cloves, crushed

1 onion, finely diced

2 red peppers, deseeded and cut into thick chunks

400g tin cherry tomatoes, chopped

3 tbsp sundried tomato paste

175g quinoa, washed and drained

75g red lentils

350ml vegetable stock

400g tin cannellini or butter beans, drained

2 tsp dried oregano

2 tsp dried parsley

1 tsp rosemary

seasoning, to taste

1 courgette, thickly diced

fresh parsley, to garnish

It is important to get enough protein when you are vegan. The only food, other than animal products, that offers a complete form of protein is quinoa. It is a seed but more of a pseudo-grain really. I have added it into a delicious tomato and vegetable base here, boosting its nutritional value, taste and texture. I throw some red lentils or beans into many of my vegan dishes, again to increase the nutritional value.

1 Preheat your slow cooker following the manufacturer's instructions.

2 Place all the ingredients (apart from the courgette, if you want it to be al dente, and the fresh parsley garnish) into your slow cooker. Season to taste.

3 Cook on low for 4–5 hours or on high for 3 hours.

4 One hour before serving, add the courgette, turn to high (if you haven't already) and cook to help soften the courgette.

5 Serve with a garnish of fresh parsley.

6 This dish is nice served hot or cold.

NOTE

I really dislike soft courgette, so I add it in the last hour of cooking. You can however add this earlier if you wish.

GARLIC POTATO & GRUYÈRE LAYER CAKE

SERVES 4–6

If you like homity pie or cheese pies, you will love this. It is great as a summer lunch, or even as a packed lunch as it holds its shape perfectly when sliced.

1 Line your slow cooker with baking parchment, slow cooker liner or a cake liner. If you prefer you can grease it well with butter, but if your slow cooker has a tendency to catch in places, I urge you to line it.

2 Preheat your slow cooker following the manufacturer's instructions.

3 Once you have all the ingredients prepared, it is simply a matter of layering. I start with the potato, add some onion and garlic, and then Gruyère cheese, and continue layering in this order until all the main ingredients have been used.

4 Mix the eggs with the double cream, add in the herbs and Parmesan, combine well and pour this over the layers.

5 Place a tea towel under the lid to help absorb any moisture. Cook on high for 2½ hours. If your slow cooker is a little on the hot side, opt instead to cook this on low for 5–6 hours, or until the potatoes are cooked through.

6 Serve with baked beans or a salad.

NUTRITIONAL INFORMATION PER SERVING

771 Kcals

55g fat

33g net carbohydrates

33g protein

INGREDIENTS

3 potatoes, peeled and very thinly sliced

1 large onion, thinly sliced

3–4 garlic cloves, crushed

200g vegetarian Gruyère cheese, grated

6 large eggs, beaten

200ml double cream

1 tsp oregano or mixed Italian herbs

100g vegetarian Parmesan cheese, grated

VEGAN COWBOY BEANS

SERVES 4

NUTRITIONAL INFORMATION PER SERVING

386 Kcals

11g fat

40g net carbohydrates

22g protein

INGREDIENTS

1 tsp olive oil or coconut oil

2 star anise

1 large red onion, chopped

2 garlic cloves, crushed

1–2 chillies (to taste), finely chopped

1–2 tsp chilli powder (or to taste)

1 red pepper, deseeded and diced

2 tsp smoked paprika

1 tsp marjoram

¼ tsp cayenne pepper

400g tin chopped tomatoes

2 tbsp sundried tomato paste

50g red lentils

2 x 400g tins large haricot beans (use mixed beans if you prefer)

350ml vegetable stock

fresh parsley, to garnish

Unlike a lot of vegetarian spiced chillies, this recipe is more like a lush version of baked beans with a spicy kick. It is perfect to enhance a vegan breakfast, eaten as a fast lunch with some crusty bread, or as a main meal served with rice, tacos and guacamole dip.

1 Preheat your slow cooker following the manufacturer's instructions.

2 Heat the olive oil or coconut oil in pan on the hob, on a medium heat. Add the star anise, onions, garlic, chilli and pepper. If you have a sauté facility on your slow cooker, you can use this. Sauté gently until starting to soften slightly.

3 Remove the star anise.

4 Transfer to the slow cooker. Add all remaining ingredients and combine well.

5 Cook on low for 4–5 hours.

6 Garnish with fresh parsley and serve with brown basmati rice, or, for reduced carbs, cauliflower rice and some sour cream on the side.

MEDITERRANEAN BULGUR WHEAT RISOTTO

Bulgur wheat cooks quickly and is great to make a version of risotto. It works so well with Mediterranean flavours. I have added some lentils here to balance the protein. This can also be served as a cold lunch; it is delicious topped with some crushed cashews and, if you are vegetarian rather than vegan, some crumbled feta cheese.

1 Preheat your slow cooker following the manufacturer's instructions.

2 Place all the ingredients, apart from the bulgur wheat, into your slow cooker and cook on high for 2–2½ hours.

3 Add the bulgur wheat and stir well. Season to taste and continue to cook for another 30 minutes, or until the bulgur wheat is cooked to your taste.

4 Stir well and serve with chopped cashew nuts, or if vegetarian, some crumbled feta cheese.

NUTRITIONAL INFORMATION PER SERVING

351 Kcals

11g fat

47g net carbohydrates

12g protein

INGREDIENTS

1 small onion, finely diced

2 garlic cloves, finely diced

1 red pepper, deseeded and diced

1 aubergine, diced

2 tsp dried oregano

1 tsp dried thyme

3 tbsp sundried tomato paste

400g tin chopped tomatoes

75g red lentils

400ml hot vegetable stock

150g bulgur wheat

seasoning, to taste

CHICKPEA CURRY

SERVES 4

NUTRITIONAL INFORMATION PER SERVING

591 Kcals

33g fat

45g net carbohydrates

20g protein

INGREDIENTS

1 onion, diced

3 garlic cloves, crushed

2 red chillies, diced

3cm piece fresh ginger, grated

½ tsp ground cinnamon

1 tsp ground cardamom

1–2 tbsp garam masala

1 tsp ground coriander

½ tsp ground cumin

1 tsp ground turmeric

400g tin chopped tomatoes

2 tbsp tomato purée

2 x 400g tins chickpeas, drained

150g creamed coconut

chopped coriander, to garnish

Chickpeas are so versatile, and packed with protein, calcium, magnesium and fibre. This is a very simple chickpea curry. I love adding handfuls of spinach (frozen or fresh). If I have cauliflower, I may add this as the cauliflower and chickpea combo is delicious. Just like any spiced dish, the flavours enhance when left for a while, so this is a perfect meal to cook the day before serving. It also freezes well.

1 Preheat your slow cooker following the manufacturer's instructions.

2 Add all the ingredients and combine well.

3 Cook on low for 4–5 hours.

4 Garnish with chopped coriander and serve with basmati rice and naan breads.

ALOO GOBI

This is a fantastic Indian dish and very cheap to produce. It is also a tasty alternative to a meat-based curry. It is nice and mild, so perfect for families. I like to double up and freeze all my curries, so I end up with individual portions of several varieties of curry ready for the perfect 'fakeaway' night without any effort.

1 Add the oil, garlic, ginger, spices, tomatoes and chillies (if using) to your food processor and whizz until a paste is formed.

2 Chop the potatoes into chunks so they are roughly all the same size as the cauliflower florets.

3 Preheat your slow cooker following the manufacturer's instructions.

4 Place the potatoes, cauliflower, onion and coconut cream in the slow cooker. Pour on the paste and the stock/water, and combine well.

5 Cook on low for 6–8 hours.

6 Thirty minutes before serving, add the spinach and nigella seeds. If the mix is too thick, add some more stock or water. If you need to thicken, mix a heaped teaspoon of cornflour with some water to form a paste and stir it in. Turn to high and continue to cook for 30 minutes.

7 Serve with basmati rice garnished with nigella seeds or, for a healthier side, with cauliflower or broccoli rice.

NUTRITIONAL INFORMATION PER SERVING

321 Kcals

14g fat

36g net carbohydrates

9.1g protein

INGREDIENTS

2 tbsp olive oil

2 garlic cloves

2–3cm piece fresh ginger

2 tbsp korma curry powder (if you want it mild) or opt for garam masala

½ tsp cumin

½ tsp ground turmeric

¼ tsp nutmeg

2–3 tomatoes

1–2 green chillies, diced (optional)

2–3 large potatoes, peeled and diced

1 cauliflower, cut into small florets

1 large red onion, diced

250ml coconut cream

200ml vegetable stock or water

80g spinach

½ tsp nigella seeds, plus extra for garnishing

heaped tsp cornflour (if needed)

8

You don't always think about your slow cooker when making side dishes, but you would be surprised at how much you can do. My favourite is Dauphinoise Potatoes (page 147), especially served with my Beef Bourguignon (page 66).

ROAST POTATOES

SERVES 4

NUTRITIONAL INFORMATION PER SERVING

581 Kcals

43g fat

41g net carbohydrates

4.7g protein

INGREDIENTS

4–5 large potatoes, peeled and cut to size (I use Maris Pipers)

2 tbsp goose fat or olive oil

1 tbsp semolina

1 tsp paprika

seasoning, to taste

You may not have ever thought of doing roast potatoes in the slow cooker, but – yes! – you can make delicious roasties with this versatile appliance. These are good when you don't want to use your main oven – for example, I cook them this way when I am making a main dish on the hob. I have also had friends use this recipe at Christmas when a turkey is taking up all the room in the oven.

1 Preheat your slow cooker following the manufacturer's instructions.

2 Parboil your potatoes until the edges are soft and starting to go fluffy. Drain in a colander and leave to sit to dry out slightly.

3 Heat your slow cooker on high for 10 minutes. If you have a multi-cooker, you can switch to sauté to heat up the pan, but remember to switch this back to slow cooker mode once the temperature is reached.

4 Pour in the fat or oil and allow to melt. Add the potatoes and toss until the oil covers them. You can add a little more oil if needed, but the potatoes only need a coating of oil, not to be absorbed in it.

5 Mix together the semolina, paprika and seasoning, and sprinkle over the potatoes.

6 Place a tea towel under the cooker lid to absorb any moisture. Cook on high for 3–4 hours until crispy. You can turn the potatoes two or three times during cooking, but always replace the tea towel under the lid and ensure you have a good seal to stop the heat evaporating.

7 Serve when crispy.

DAUPHINOISE POTATOES

I love the creaminess of dauphinoise potatoes and serve them with my slow-cooked Beef Bourguignon (page 66), which I make the day before as it always benefits from spending a day in the fridge before reheating to help deepen the flavours. The other advantage of doing this is that it frees up my slow cooker for the dauphinoise!

1 Preheat your slow cooker following the manufacturer's instructions.

2 In a saucepan, add the cream, milk and garlic. Season to taste. Place on a medium heat and bring up to a simmer.

3 Add the sliced potatoes and allow to cook for 5 minutes, stirring occasionally.

4 Gently scoop out the potatoes and layer them into your slow cooker. Pour on the remaining cream mixture. Finish with a sprinkle of Gruyère cheese if desired.

5 Pop a tea towel under the lid to absorb any moisture.

6 Cook on low for 4–5 hours until the potatoes are nice and tender.

NUTRITIONAL INFORMATION PER SERVING

594 Kcals

48g fat

28g net carbohydrates

9.7g protein

INGREDIENTS

500ml double cream

200ml whole milk

3–4 garlic cloves, crushed

seasoning, to taste

6 large potatoes, finely sliced (I use Maris Pipers)

100g vegetarian Gruyère cheese (optional)

fresh dill, to garnish

JACKET POTATOES

SERVES 4

NUTRITIONAL INFORMATION
PER SERVING

179 Kcals

3.4g fat

38g net carbohydrates

4.1g protein

INGREDIENTS

4 baking potatoes, washed

1 tbsp olive oil

sea salt

With the cost of electricity so high at the moment, you may be thinking twice about turning on your oven to cook some jacket potatoes. Fear not, the slow cooker makes perfect jackets with ease.

1 Preheat your slow cooker following the manufacturer's instructions.

2 Wash the potatoes.

3 Brush with olive oil before adding sea salt.

4 Place baking parchment in the base of your slow cooker to prevent the jackets sticking to the base. Add the jacket potatoes.

5 Place a tea towel under the lid to absorb moisture.

6 Cook on low for 7–8 hours.

TOP TIP

I love to cook mine in the slow cooker, then when cooked, scoop out the middle, mix it with cheese, chives, spring onion, cream cheese and diced ham or cooked bacon, pop it all back into the jacket and place on high in the slow cooker for another hour. Delicious!

HOT LUXURY POTATO SALAD

SERVES 4

I love this recipe because you can add anything you wish, but it works brilliantly with new potatoes, spring onions, garlic and bacon. You can also finish with a generous cheese topping. If you are vegetarian, you can, of course, omit the bacon.

1 Preheat your slow cooker following the manufacturer's instructions.

2 Place the potatoes in a bowl, add the melted butter or olive oil and toss well until evenly covered.

3 Place in the slow cooker along with all the ingredients apart from the spring onions and cheese.

4 Place a tea towel under the lid to prevent moisture. Cook on high for 3–4 hours until the potatoes are cooked and the bacon is starting to crisp.

5 When ready to serve, place in a large serving dish. Stir in the spring onions and cheese until evenly coated.

6 Serve immediately.

NUTRITIONAL INFORMATION PER SERVING

564 Kcals

33g fat

38g net carbohydrates

2g protein

INGREDIENTS

1kg bag new potatoes, halved or quartered

2 tbsp melted butter or olive oil

6 rashers back bacon, diced

3–4 garlic cloves, thinly sliced

generous serving sea salt

generous serving black pepper

2 tsp paprika

1 tsp dried oregano

1 bunch spring onions, finely sliced

PEASE PUDDING

SERVES 4

NUTRITIONAL INFORMATION PER SERVING

129 Kcals

0.8g fat

19g net carbohydrates

8.9g protein

INGREDIENTS

350g yellow split peas (soak overnight if using dried)

3 garlic cloves, crushed

750ml boiling water (more if needed)

I was a vegetarian for many years and this was a real family favourite. We used to have it with a roast, but traditionally it is served with thick chunks of ham/gammon (see page 96 for my Cider-Infused Gammon). Pease pudding is also known as pease porridge. You may remember the rhyme, 'Pease porridge hot, pease porridge cold, pease porridge in the pot, nine days old'. It is very simple to make and can be stored in an airtight container in the fridge and used as a nourishing side dish, perhaps as an alternative to mashed potato.

1 Preheat your slow cooker following the manufacturer's instructions.

2 Place all the ingredients into your slow cooker. Combine well.

3 Cook on low for 6–8 hours until the water is absorbed and the split peas have softened.

4 Using a metal potato masher, gently mash the split peas. They should start to form a nice mash. Add more water if you need to.

5 If you plan to reheat this later, you may need to add a little more water to help soften it.

TOP TIP

I would suggest you use a slow cooker liner and always cook on low as it can catch on some older slow cooker models.

CORN ON THE COB

SERVES 4

I used to feel very grown up when we had this as children. My mum had these fancy sticks for us to hold them with to avoid mess, while butter dribbled down our chins. You may not have thought about doing these in the slow cooker, but it is so easy and enhances the flavour.

You will need enough tinfoil to wrap each individual corn on the cob.

1 Preheat your slow cooker following the manufacturer's instructions.

2 Cut the tinfoil big enough to wrap up each individual corn on the cob. I prefer to wrap them individually as I have found doing them in one large parcel can result in some corn not having any butter while others are overwhelmed.

3 Place a corn on the cob in the centre of each tinfoil sheet. Add approximately 1 tablespoon of butter, randomly dolloped onto each corn, and season generously with black pepper and salt.

4 Wrap each foil parcel, folding tightly at the ends to avoid the butter seeping out when melted. Place each parcel into the slow cooker.

5 Cook on high for approximately 2 hours. If you prefer, you can cook on low for 4–5 hours.

TOP TIP

Thinking of doing corn on the cob for a BBQ? You can cook the corn in your slow cooker and then place it on your BBQ to char slightly before serving.

NUTRITIONAL INFORMATION PER SERVING

99 Kcals

8.2g fat

4.2g net carbohydrates

1.5g protein

INGREDIENTS

4 corn on the cob

4 tbsp butter

black pepper

salt

9

We don't always think of making desserts in the slow cooker, but they are delicious and so easy. The slow cooker can be used to make delicious puddings, desserts and even cakes. I love slow cooking so much I have a separate small slow cooker I use only for desserts.

If you are new to slow cooking, I strongly advise you to read the following advice on how the slow cooker works for desserts and sponge puddings. This is really important to ensure success.

DIETARY SWAPS

We are all becoming increasingly health conscious. Using gluten-free, vegan or sugar-free alternatives can often mean that a recipe does not work as well as the original, but here are my top tips to convert any recipe to your preferred way of eating …

GLUTEN-FREE

We have some fantastic gluten-free flours available now. You can literally swap like for like and still get great results, though I have found that adding around 30ml more liquid when using gluten-free flour in cakes and sponge puddings gives much better results. Some dessert recipes contain suet – you will need to check the labels but you can buy gluten-free and vegetarian suet.

VEGAN

You can buy vegan margarines that work as a direct swap for butter. You can also use coconut oil. To replace animal milks, switch to almond, coconut or rice milk. For eggs, you can buy an egg replacement, but I use my own version, mixing 1 tablespoon of flax or chia seeds with equal

▶▶▶

amounts of water, leaving to soak and then using this as a binder. You can also use nut butters, stewed fruit or mashed banana. Cashews are very good for vegan cooking as they can be soaked to form a very creamy base, ideal for desserts or even soups. Some dessert recipes use suet, but you can opt for vegetarian suet.

SUGAR-FREE

This book is not following any diet plan and therefore has no restrictions in terms of fats, carbs or sugars. Many of you may already know that this is my passion and I have already written several books on sugar-free diets. I have worked with more than 35 schools, reducing sugar intake by 40% in cakes and desserts without anyone noticing any changes. You really don't need things to be very sweet, so please bear this in mind when you are using these recipes. You can reduce the sweetness to suit your palate as you become more used to fewer sweet foods. Start gradually and reduce, allowing you and your family to get used to fewer sweet foods, therefore reducing sweet cravings.

You can also opt for natural sweeteners that don't spike your blood sugar and are low in fructose, such as erythritol, xylitol, monk fruit granules and stevia. Erythritol also comes as an icing sugar replacement, in 'brown sugar' form and in syrups (known as fibre syrup). You can also use stevia in granule or liquid form, but it is more than 300 times sweeter than sugar, so can be hard to gauge to taste. If you are reducing your sugar intake, remember that the natural sugars found in bananas, dates, dried fruit, fruit juices, honey, maple syrup, agave, coconut sugar, and so on, are all still packed with glucose and fructose, so using them is only a sideways step. You will need to cut down on these, or avoid them altogether, in order to keep your blood sugar low.

For more information and great recipes, check out my website: www.everydaysugarfree.co.uk

FAT

The following recipes suggest using butter or margarine. I am a fan of butter as I prefer natural foods and butter is not as inflammatory as man-made fats, but you can opt for whatever suits your budget and health objectives. I am also a huge fan of the low-carb way of eating, where we keep our fats high and our carbs and sugars very low. You can look at reducing sugar/carb content by making some swaps to natural sweeteners and switching flour to a nut-based flour such as ground almonds or coconut flour.

HOW TO GET A PUDDING BOWL IN AND OUT OF THE SLOW COOKER

A slow cooker is great for making puddings, but it can be tricky getting them in and out of it without burning yourself. To avoid such accidents, you can make yourself an easy string handle or a foil strap.

String handle If I am using string to tie the top of a basin, I cut a second piece, around 40cm long, and double it over. I then loop it around the string tied either side of the top of the basin and tie it in the middle to form a handle.

Foil strap Simply select a sheet of foil big enough to fit around the pudding basin and give you enough to hold on to – I usually opt for around 40–50cm. Fold the foil lengthways until you have a strong strap around 5cm wide. Place the bowl in the centre of the strap and fold any excess over the top. Transfer the bowl to your slow cooker and, when you need to remove it, simply unfold the strap and lift out.

TRADITIONAL RICE PUDDING

SERVES 6

NUTRITIONAL INFORMATION PER SERVING

374 Kcals

26g fat

27g net carbohydrates

7.1g protein

INGREDIENTS

1 litre whole milk

3 tbsp sugar

80g pudding rice

1 cinnamon stick

1 tbsp butter (plus extra for greasing the bowl)

200ml double cream

sprinkle of nutmeg, to garnish

I get cravings for milky pudding whenever I feel under par – it really is the ultimate comfort pudding. I love to add cinnamon to my rice pudding, but you can omit this if you prefer. To vary the flavour, why not try adding 15 crushed cardamom seeds along with the sugar (you can also use three or four pods and remove the outer skin after crushing), or using coconut cream instead of double cream?

1 Grease the slow cooker bowl with butter.

2 Preheat your slow cooker following the manufacturer's instructions.

3 Place the milk, sugar, rice and cinnamon stick in the slow cooker. Dot with the butter.

4 Cook on low for 5–6 hours. Remember to stir every now and again as the rice may stick or cook in lumps otherwise.

5 Once cooked, remove the cinnamon stick. Add the cream and cook on high for a further 15 minutes, stirring occasionally. Add more milk if needed until you get the consistency you desire.

6 Serve as is, with a sprinkle of nutmeg.

VEGANS

If you are vegan, you could swap the butter for vegan butter, swap the milk for coconut milk, and add a carton of vegan cream to create a creamy consistency and flavour.

GRANDMA'S SYRUP PUDDING

SERVES 8

I called this grandma's, but I am probably deceiving you. My nan was a terrible cook; her talents lay in making us all laugh – I miss her every day. This is a very traditional steamed pudding, oozing with syrupy sweetness and a slightly lemony sponge. It is best enjoyed with home-made custard.

You will need a 1.2 litre pudding basin, parchment, foil and string, or you can use small basins as shown in the photo.

1 Preheat your slow cooker following the manufacturer's instructions.

2 Grease your pudding bowl thoroughly with butter.

3 Place the golden syrup in the base of the bowl. Add the breadcrumbs and give it a quick, gentle stir to ensure it is combined.

4 Cream the butter and sugar together in a mixing bowl. Add the eggs, beat well and follow with the sifted flour.

5 Add the lemon zest and juice. Stir well. Add the milk and combine.

6 Place the mixture into your pudding basin. Cover the pudding basin with parchment and a layer of foil and tie very securely with string. I like to use a double-sided parchment with foil on one side and parchment on the other. It is advisable to make a handle with string (see page 159), to make it easier to lift the pudding in and out of the slow cooker.

7 Boil the kettle. Place the pudding in the base of your slow cooker. Add enough boiling water until it comes halfway up the sides of the pudding bowl.

8 Cook on low for 4–6 hours, on high for 2–3 hours, or until the sponge springs back when touched. If you are using small bowls, the sponge will cook slightly quicker.

9 Remove from the slow cooker. Run a knife around the edge of the bowl. Place a plate on the top of the bowl and carefully flip it to turn out the pudding.

10 Serve immediately with home-made custard.

NUTRITIONAL INFORMATION PER SERVING

428 Kcals

21g fat

53g net carbohydrates

6.4g protein

INGREDIENTS

5 tbsp golden syrup

60g fine breadcrumbs

175g butter (plus extra for greasing the bowl)

150g sugar

3 large eggs

200g self-raising flour

1 large lemon, zest and juice

2 tbsp milk

SIMPLE BERRY CRUMBLE

NUTRITIONAL INFORMATION PER SERVING

704 Kcals

34g fat

89g net carbohydrates

7.5g protein

INGREDIENTS

200g frozen mixed berries, defrosted

70g sugar

3 tbsp water

FOR THE CRUMBLE TOPPING

100g plain flour

150g oats (or muesli)

100g sugar

150g butter

I have included various crumble recipes in my other slow cooker books, but this is one of the fastest and, in my view, tastiest. I like to make them in small ramekins, perfect for breakfasts as well as desserts. I am a bit rough and ready with the crumble mix, as I often use anything I can find in the cupboard, from oats right through to any leftover muesli or granola. I have been more restrained in this recipe, but do feel free to experiment.

1 Preheat your slow cooker following the manufacturer's instructions.

2 Place the defrosted berries in a bowl, add the sugar and water and combine.

3 Place in the ramekins until they are half full.

4 Prepare your crumble topping by mixing the flour, oats and sugar together before rubbing in the cold butter until the mixture resembles breadcrumbs.

5 Place the crumble over the berry mixture.

6 Put the ramekins in your slow cooker. Place a tea towel under the lid to help absorb any moisture.

7 Cook on low for 2 hours.

8 Serve with home-made custard.

DOUBLE UP AND FREEZE

You can double up this recipe and use the remaining stewed fruit to make another crumble to pop into the freezer.

JAM ROLY-POLY

SERVES 4–6

When thinking about comforting desserts, I am always transported back to my childhood – the traditional recipes, with cheap and cheerful but very filling desserts, instead of the processed snacks we are given today. Jam roly-poly was one of my dad's favourites; he loved a suet-style pudding – sweet or savoury!

1 Preheat your slow cooker following the manufacturer's instructions.

2 Place the flour, sugar, suet and lemon zest into a bowl.

3 Add the milk a little at a time until it forms a nice dough – you may not need all of it. Form the dough into a sausage and place onto a lightly floured board.

4 Gently roll out until you form a rectangle, approximately 15cm x 25cm and about 1cm thick.

5 Spread the dough with a nice thick layer of raspberry jam.

6 Gently roll the dough, starting at the longest side, until it forms a sausage. Place onto a large sheet of foil and wrap loosely to allow expansion but with sealed ends.

7 Place a rack on the base of your slow cooker. Place the foil parcel onto the rack. Add boiling water to the slow cooker until it reaches the tinfoil base, but no higher. You want the steam, not the water, to cook the roly-poly.

8 Cook on high for 2–3 hours.

9 Remove carefully and unwrap. Cut into thick slices and serve with home-made custard, ice cream or crème fraîche.

NOTE

You can use vegetarian suet if you prefer.

NUTRITIONAL INFORMATION PER SERVING

497 Kcals

15g fat

81g net carbohydrates

6.6g protein

INGREDIENTS

300g self-raising flour

100g sugar

100g shredded suet

zest of 3 lemons (unwaxed)

150–200ml milk

200g raspberry jam

SWEET BERRY PAVLOVA

SERVES 4

NUTRITIONAL INFORMATION PER SERVING

318 Kcals

25g fat

17g net carbohydrates

4.6g protein

INGREDIENTS

6 egg whites

75g caster sugar

1 tsp cream of tartar

1 tsp cornflour

FOR THE FILLING

300g thick double cream, whipped if desired

1 tsp vanilla bean paste (optional)

300g sliced banana and mixed berries of your choice

icing sugar, or mint leaves and edible gold leaf, to decorate

TOP TIP

Save the egg yolks to make Lemon & Lime Curd (page 200). You can also use them to make your own mayonnaise or custard.

I can never resist a good pavlova; it is one of my absolute favourite desserts. Light, with a chewy middle and a slight crunch to the meringue, served with thick vanilla cream and berries. What could be better? You can, of course, opt for any fruit topping you wish, but I don't think you can beat berries. I use sliced banana and defrosted frozen raspberries for the centre, and top with fresh blueberries and strawberries. I find the frozen berries give more flavour, plus the juice oozes into the cream for a delicious sweetness.

1 Preheat your slow cooker following the manufacturer's instructions.

2 Ensure you have a very clean bowl, then separate the egg yolks from the whites (retain the egg yolks for use in another recipe). Please note that egg whites will not whisk if there is any fat in the batch, so if even a tiny bit of egg yolk has crept in, you will have to start again.

3 Whisk the egg whites until they form soft peaks. Gradually add in the sugar, cream of tartar and cornflour. The whites should be stiff enough for you to be able to turn the bowl upside down and they stay put.

4 Line the slow cooker with parchment or a cake liner. Spoon the meringue mix into the slow cooker and spread. You want to maintain height around the edge and a dip in the middle, almost like a bird's nest, ready to fill with your cream and fruit when cooked.

5 Place a tea towel under the lid to help absorb any moisture. Cook on low for 2 hours until the meringue is firm to touch.

6 Once cooked, keep in the slow cooker until completely cold. Remove very carefully as it can be quite fragile.

7 Place onto a serving dish.

8 Mix the thick or whipped double cream with the vanilla. Add the cream to the base and top with your chosen fruit.

9 Decorate with a sprinkling of icing sugar or, for a lovely effect, add some mint leaves and some edible gold leaf.

MUM'S SIMPLE BREAD & BUTTER PUDDING

SERVES 6

My mum used to make this for us when we were children as it is a very cheap and cheerful pudding, great for using up leftover bread, milk and eggs, and it is still one of my favourite comfort foods, so I had to add it to this book. It cooks well in the slow cooker, but does benefit from being browned in the oven or under the grill before serving if, like me, you love the crisp edges to contrast with the soft, sweet centre of the pudding. If your slow cooker inner is ovenproof, you can simply cook it in the slow cooker base and then lift it out to brown in the oven or under the grill.

1 Butter the base of your slow cooker or, if using one, your ovenproof dish (make sure it fits inside the slow cooker).

2 Preheat your slow cooker following the manufacturer's instructions.

3 Mix together the milk, eggs, orange zest and mixed spice.

4 Layer the buttered bread in your base or dish, sprinkling with the sultanas and a fine sprinkle of sugar as you go. Pour over the milk mixture.

5 Place a tea towel under the lid of the slow cooker to contain any moisture. Cook on low for 3–4 hours.

6 You can serve immediately, but if you prefer a very crispy top, place in a preheated oven (around 180°C) or under the grill to brown the top until crispy and golden.

7 Serve with a dollop of cream, crème fraîche or Greek yoghurt.

TOP TIP

You can use any bread, including stale bread, fruit breads, hot cross buns or even leftover Christmas panettone. You can also vary the flavours, using chocolate chips, raspberries, banana or chunks of apple.

NUTRITIONAL INFORMATION PER SERVING

343 Kcals

9g fat

51g net carbohydrates

13g protein

INGREDIENTS

butter, for greasing

500ml whole milk

3 large eggs

1 orange, zest only

1 tsp mixed spice

10 slices of white bread (or other bread of your choice), can be slightly stale, buttered

100g sultanas

50g sugar

SPICED TOFFEE APPLE & ALMOND CRUMBLE

SERVES 4–6

NUTRITIONAL INFORMATION
PER SERVING

678 Kcals

31g fat

85g net carbohydrates

13g protein

INGREDIENTS

75ml boiling water

100g brown sugar

2 tbsp golden syrup

30g butter

4 cooking apples (approx. 600g),
peeled and diced

60g sultanas

1 tsp ground cinnamon

1 tsp mixed spice

FOR THE CRUMBLE TOPPING

150g plain flour

100g butter

150g oats

80g ground almonds

50g flaked almonds

75g brown sugar

1 tsp ground cinnamon

I love this dish, but it should come with a sugar warning! It has a bit more pizzazz than your standard family crumble and is wonderful when served with some vanilla ice cream – a real dinner-party wow pud!

1 Place the boiling water, sugar, syrup and butter in the base of your slow cooker. Turn on to high (or if you have a multi-cooker, turn to sauté) and heat until the sugar has melted.

2 Add the apples, along with the sultanas and spices, and ensure they are coated well in the mixture. Cook on high for 1 hour.

3 Meanwhile, make the crumble topping, rubbing the butter into the flour until it resembles breadcrumbs. Add the remaining crumble ingredients.

4 Place the crumble mixture over the apples. Place a tea towel under the lid to help absorb any moisture. Continue to cook on low for 3 hours.

5 Serve with a dollop of vanilla ice cream.

CINNAMON & BERRY BRIOCHE PUDDING

I am a big fan of bread & butter-style puddings, but this takes it to a whole other level. The brioche is baked in a cinnamon and vanilla base interspersed with berries (I use frozen mixed berry mix, but you can use any berry combination). This is lovely served with some double cream.

1 Preheat your slow cooker following the manufacturer's instructions.

2 Place the brioche pieces into ramekin dishes, alternating with the berries.

3 Put the remaining ingredients in a large jug and beat until combined.

4 Pour the egg mixture over the brioche. You may need to keep pushing down the bread until all the mixture is absorbed.

5 Place the ramekins in the base of the slow cooker and turn on to low. Cook for 1½–2½ hours until cooked. The egg base must be firm to touch.

6 Remove from the slow cooker and serve immediately with a swirl of double cream or a dollop of ice cream.

NUTRITIONAL INFORMATION PER SERVING

661 Kcals

60g fat

16g net carbohydrates

11g protein

INGREDIENTS

4–5 brioche rolls, cut into quarters

100g frozen mixed berries

400ml double cream

2 tsp cinnamon

1 pinch ground or freshly grated nutmeg

2 tsp vanilla extract

4 large eggs, beaten

10

If you are new to slow cooking, I strongly urge you to read the following advice on how the slow cooker works for bread and cakes. This is really important to ensure success.

CAKES AND SPONGES

Cakes and sponges will not have the same light texture as they do when baked, but they can be just as delicious. A slow cooker can sometimes get quite wet inside, especially with all the moisture that accumulates. To prevent this from affecting your cakes or sponges, simply place a tea towel over the top of the slow cooker before replacing the lid, and push down firmly to ensure it forms a good seal. This technique is also helpful when you want to achieve a drier, crispy edge to your food. It is not necessary to use a tea towel if you are slow cooking a pudding with a foil/parchment lid.

HOW TO PREVENT BURNING

Some slow cookers give an uneven heat or cook at a higher temperature than others. If you are cooking a cake or dessert with a long, slow cook, you can add a foil collar to prevent the edges of the cake from catching. It is very simple: just make a long sausage of foil and place this around the edge of the base of the slow cooker. You can then put cake liners into the slow cooker, or use silicon cake tins if your prefer, and it will prevent the edges from catching.

DIETARY SWAPS

Please see the Desserts section (page 157) for information about gluten-free, vegan, sugar-free and low-fat alternatives.

CINNAMON & ORANGE BUNS

MAKES APPROX. 8 BUNS

NUTRITIONAL INFORMATION
PER SERVING

423 Kcals

5.2g fat

84g net carbohydrates

8g protein

INGREDIENTS
FOR THE DOUGH

500g strong white bread flour,
plus extra for dusting

40g sugar

7g sachet fast-acting yeast

200ml milk

150ml hot water

40g butter, melted

1 tsp salt

FOR THE FILLING

75g brown sugar

zest and juice of 1 large orange

3 tsp ground cinnamon

FOR THE ICING GLAZE

200g icing sugar

1–2 tbsp cold water

There is nothing like a cinnamon and orange bun drizzled in icing. Slow cooker buns do come out a little paler than their oven-baked counterparts, however it is purely a matter of aesthetics. You can, of course, darken them by placing them in the oven or under the grill until golden, but as you will be covering them with lashings of icing, it really doesn't matter!

1 Place your bread flour and sugar in a bowl and add the yeast.

2 Place the milk and hot water in a jug (this will create a warm liquid; it must not be too hot but body temperature, approx. 36°C). Add the butter and combine well. Pour this mixture into your bowl of flour, add the salt and mix well until combined into a dough.

3 You need to knead the dough for at least 10 minutes. You can use your hands, or you can use the bread dough hook attachment on a mixer. If you are not used to kneading, you put a small amount of flour on your worktop, place the dough on top and work it with a fold-and-turn motion. As you progress, your dough should become nice and pliable and not too sticky, but it is better for it to be slightly wet than too dry. Add more water if your dough is dry and crumbling.

4 When you've achieved the right consistency, roll out the dough into a rectangle, approximately 20cm x 30cm.

5 In a bowl, mix together the brown sugar, orange zest and juice and cinnamon, and spread this over the dough.

6 Working with the longest edge, roll the dough to form one long sausage. Cut this into eight pieces, each of roughly 3–4cm thickness.

7 Line the slow cooker with baking parchment. Remember to use a foil collar (see page 177) before adding the liner if your machine has a tendency to burn or overheat. Add the cinnamon buns until you have covered the base. Don't worry if they are touching – they will cook into one large piece and you can pull them apart when cooked.

8 Place a tea towel under the lid of the slow cooker. Cook on high for 2 hours, or until the buns are cooked. Carefully lift out the buns using the parchment to help you.

9 If you want to add a little more colour to the buns when cooked, you can place them under the grill for a few minutes.

10 Mix the icing sugar with a little cold water at a time and stir well until it achieves a thick consistency. Drizzle this over the buns. I leave the buns in one piece and let the family pull them apart when they need to, but you can separate them before icing if you prefer.

LUXURY FRUIT CAKE

SERVES 10

This is a very easy, moist fruit cake. It's perfect for everyday use, but can also serve as a Christmas or Easter cake. If I am making a Christmas cake, I soak my fruit in 200ml of brandy overnight and, once the cake is cooked, I store it in an airtight tin and feed it with more brandy every few weeks (I make some holes in the top with a skewer and drizzle with a tablespoon or two of brandy), to add extra flavour before decorating.

1 Place all the dried fruit into a bowl and add the cold tea or brandy and the orange zest and juice. Leave overnight to absorb the liquid (or leave for 1 hour if you're in a hurry).

2 Beat the sugar and butter together in a bowl until light and fluffy. Add the black treacle and combine, then add the eggs, one at a time, alternating with a spoonful of sieved flour/spices. Continue until all the flour and spices have been combined into the mixture.

3 Fold in the fruit mixture and add the flaked almonds.

4 If your slow cooker has enough space for you to put your cake tin inside it, you can just line the cake tin and put this inside your slow cooker. Some silicon cake tins fit well in the slow cooker (I use these). If not, place a rolled-up collar of foil (see page 177) around the edge of your slow cooker. Follow this with a triple cake liner (to add more strength so the cake will hold its shape) and then add the cake mixture.

5 Ensure the cake batter is level.

6 Place a tea towel under the lid of the slow cooker and cook on low for 6–8 hours (timings will depend on your machine, so check if the cake is cooked by poking a skewer into it – if it comes out clean, it is cooked).

7 Carefully remove the cake from the slow cooker. Place it on a cooling rack and leave until cool.

8 Store in an airtight container ready to eat or decorate.

NUTRITIONAL INFORMATION PER SERVING

632 Kcals

24g fat

92g net carbohydrates

9g protein

INGREDIENTS

750g mixed dried fruit

80g dried cherries

200ml cold tea (or brandy, if preferred)

zest and juice of 1 orange

175g soft brown sugar

200g butter

1 tbsp black treacle

3 eggs, beaten

200g plain flour, sieved

1 tsp baking powder

2 tsp ground cinnamon

2 tsp ground allspice

100g flaked almonds

GOOEY CHOCOLATE BROWNIES

SERVES 6–8

NUTRITIONAL INFORMATION
PER SERVING

380 Kcals

26g fat

29g net carbohydrates

7.5g protein

INGREDIENTS

125g butter

200g dark chocolate

150g sugar

3 large eggs

185g plain flour

1 tsp baking powder

pinch salt

2 tsp vanilla extract

Chocolate brownies are a favourite of many, but you can have good and bad brownies. It is all about the cooking time. You want them to be slightly undercooked to get that gooey fudginess that is so appealing. Cook them for too long and you'll have a drier piece of chocolate cake, and the appeal of the brownie has vanished. Timings, as ever, do vary depending on your machine, as some cook quicker/higher than others.

1 Preheat your slow cooker following the manufacturer's instructions.

2 Place the butter and dark chocolate into a bowl and place this over a saucepan of boiling water (make sure the bottom of the bowl does not touch the water). You can use a bain-marie or a microwave. If you are using the latter, be very careful as the butter and chocolate can burn easily. I would advise doing it in 10–20-second bursts, stirring after each burst, and repeating until melted.

3 Meanwhile, whisk the sugar and eggs together until light and fluffy.

4 Fold the chocolate/butter mixture into the eggs/sugar before sifting in the flour and baking powder. Add the salt and vanilla extract. Fold in carefully.

5 Line the slow cooker with baking parchment. Remember to use a foil collar (see page 177) before adding the liner if your machine has a tendency to burn/overheat.

6 Place the chocolate mixture into the liner. Cook on low for 3 hours. When done, the centre should still be a bit gooey/fudgy. Remove from the slow cooker and place on a baking tray to cool, before slicing and placing in an airtight container.

7 Serve warm with a dollop of thick cream or vanilla ice cream.

TOP TIP

If your slow cooker is a tad overzealous, you can use a sausage of foil to cover the edges of the base. This helps lift the bake from the corners, which have more of a tendency to catch. Place the cake liner or parchment over this.

APPLE CAKE

SERVES 8

I love apple cake. My dad always asked me to make my spiced apple cake (full of cinnamon) as a special treat for him, but this is a milder apple cake, using dessert apples to decorate the top, but with some Bramley apple in the base, and with a vanilla and almond sponge. It is more like a dessert as it is delicious with some clotted cream or custard, but is still perfect with a cup of tea.

1 Preheat your slow cooker following the manufacturer's instructions.

1 Beat the butter and sugar together in a bowl until light and fluffy. Add the eggs, one at a time, alternating with a spoonful of sieved flour. Continue until all the flour, baking powder, ground almonds and cinnamon (if using) are combined into the mixture.

2 Fold in the vanilla extract and diced Bramley apple.

3 If your slow cooker has enough space for you to put your cake tin inside it, you can just line the cake tin and put this inside your slow cooker. Some silicon cake tins fit well in the slow cooker (I use these). If not, place a rolled-up collar of foil (see page 177) around the edge of your slow cooker. Follow this with a triple cake liner (to add more strength so the cake will hold its shape) and then add the cake mixture.

4 Ensure the cake batter is level.

5 Place the red apple slices on top to form a nice circular pattern on the cake.

6 Place a tea towel under the lid of the slow cooker and cook on low for 3–4 hours (timings will depend on your machine, so check if the cake is cooked by poking a skewer into it – if it comes out clean, it is cooked).

7 Carefully remove the cake from the slow cooker. Place it on a cooling rack and leave until cool.

8 Sprinkle with icing sugar. Store in an airtight container.

NUTRITIONAL INFORMATION PER SERVING

437 Kcals

27g fat

41g net carbohydrates

6.9g protein

INGREDIENTS

200g butter

175g sugar

3 eggs, beaten

150g plain flour, sieved

1 tsp baking powder

60g ground almonds

1–2 tsp ground cinnamon (optional)

2 tsp vanilla extract

1 Bramley apple, peeled and diced

1–2 red apples, cut into slices

icing sugar, to decorate

WHITE BREAD

NUTRITIONAL INFORMATION PER SERVING

188 Kcals

1.2g fat

36g net carbohydrates

6.9g protein

INGREDIENTS

500g strong white bread flour, plus extra for dusting

7g sachet fast-acting yeast

1 tsp runny honey

200ml milk

150ml hot water

1 tsp salt

There is nothing like the smell that comes from baking home-made bread. We don't often think of cooking bread in the slow cooker, but it works brilliantly. If you want a nice golden top as shown in the photo, you can simply place the bread under a grill for a few minutes to brown it and add a crusty edge.

1 Place your bread flour in a bowl and add the yeast.

2 Place the honey in a jug. Add the milk and hot water (this will create a warm liquid; it should be roughly body temperature, not too hot). Pour this mixture into your bowl of flour, add the salt and mix well until combined.

3 You need to knead the dough for at least 10 minutes. You can use your hands, or you can use the bread dough hook attachment on a mixer. If you are not used to kneading, you put a small amount of flour on your worktop, place the dough on top and work it with a fold-and-turn motion. As you progress, your dough should become nice and pliable and not too sticky, but it is better for it to be slightly wet than too dry. Add more water if your dough is dry and crumbling.

4 Place back into your bowl, cover with a cloth and leave for 45 minutes away from drafts and in a warm place.

5 Knock the dough back and knead again for a couple of minutes, then form it into a nice plump, round dough ball.

6 Line the slow cooker with baking parchment. Add the dough to the centre. Place a tea towel under the lid of the slow cooker. Cook on high for 2 hours, or until the bread is cooked.

7 If you want to add a little more colour or crust to the top of the bread, you can place it under the grill for a few minutes.

GARLIC, CHEESE & HERB PULL-APART BREAD

MAKES APPROX. 10 SLICES

A wonderful pull-apart cheesy garlic bread. Perfect to enjoy with some delicious home-made soup.

1 Place your bread flour in a bowl and add the yeast.

2 Place the honey in a jug. Add the milk and hot water (creating a warm liquid; roughly body temperature, not too hot). Pour this into your bowl of flour, add the salt and mix well until combined.

3 You need to knead the dough for at least 10 minutes. You can use your hands or the bread dough hook attachment on a mixer. If you are not used to kneading, you put a small amount of flour on your worktop, place the dough on top and work it with a fold-and-turn motion. As you progress, your dough should become pliable and not too sticky, but it is better to be slightly wet than too dry. Add more water if your dough is dry and crumbling.

4 Place back into your bowl, cover with a cloth and leave for 45 minutes away from drafts and in a warm place.

5 Knock the dough back and knead again for a couple of minutes, then form it into a nice plump, round dough ball.

6 Line the slow cooker with baking parchment. Add the dough to the centre. Place a tea towel under the lid of the slow cooker. Cook on high for 1 hour.

7 Lift the lid/tea towel and, keeping the bread in the slow cooker, take a sharp knife and score the top of the bread with a criss-cross pattern, which will help it to pull apart when serving.

8 Mix the Cheddar, garlic and parsley together with the cream cheese. Place the mixture over the bread, pushing into the cuts in the bread if you want it to absorb into the bread a little more. Place the tea towel back under the lid and cook for another hour.

9 If you want to add a little more colour or crust to the top of the bread, you can place it under the grill for a few minutes.

NUTRITIONAL INFORMATION PER SERVING

250 Kcals

6.5g fat

37g net carbohydrates

9.9g protein

INGREDIENTS

500g strong white bread flour, plus extra for dusting

7g sachet fast-acting yeast

1 tsp runny honey

200ml milk

150ml hot water

1 tsp salt

100g mature Cheddar cheese, grated

3–4 garlic cloves, crushed

handful freshly chopped parsley

75g cream cheese

IRISH FRUITY SODA BREAD

NUTRITIONAL INFORMATION PER SERVING

381 Kcals

2.3g fat

77g net carbohydrates

11g protein

INGREDIENTS

450g self-raising flour

1½ tsp bicarbonate of soda

40g sugar, plus extra for sprinkling

1–2 tsp cinnamon or mixed spice (optional)

½ tsp salt

50g cold butter, cut into very small pieces

100g raisins

375ml buttermilk

1 egg

Soda bread is a quick, yeast-free bread, made using baking powder and buttermilk in place of the yeast. This is a traditional Irish soda bread made sweet with raisins. This recipe also works well with dark chocolate chips. If you use a tea towel the bread can get a light tan colour but, if you want it darker, it can benefit from 1–2 minutes under the grill to create the crust and extra colour. You can also use this recipe to make a savoury soda bread, just omit the fruit and sugars – you can also add herbs, or even cheese.

1 Place the flour and bicarbonate of soda in a bowl, add the sugar, cinnamon or mixed spice (if using) and salt, and combine. Roughly rub in the cold butter before adding the raisins.

2 Place the buttermilk in a jug and add the egg, then whisk until combined. Pour this onto the flour and combine. When it starts to form a dough, tip onto a floured worktop and knead gently until it forms a firm ball of dough. If too wet, add more dough; if too dry, add a little buttermilk.

3 Shape into a round bread shape. Score the top and brush with a little buttermilk/egg mixture (I just wipe my brush around the empty jug to use up any excess), then sprinkle with some sugar.

4 Line the slow cooker with baking parchment. Add the dough to the centre. Place a tea towel under the lid of the slow cooker. Cook on high for 2–3 hours.

5 Serve sliced into chunks with plenty of butter.

BANANA & WALNUT BREAD

SERVES 8

This is the perfect way to use up overripe bananas and has the added advantage of creating a simple but delicious cake your whole family will enjoy. My slow cooker fits a loaf tin, but if yours doesn't, you can of course cook direct into the slow cooker, but don't forget to line it – not only will this make it easier to remove, but it will also prevent burning and sticking.

1 Beat the butter and sugar together until creamy. Add the bananas and eggs. Combine well before adding the flour, cinnamon and vanilla extract.

2 Once you have a creamy batter, add the walnuts and give it a final stir.

3 I use a loaf tin but, if you don't have this, I would suggest you place a triple layer of loaf-shaped cake liners into the base of your slow cooker and add the mixture. I suggest using three liners together as these will hold the mixture in shape better than just using one. You can also place the cake directly into your slow cooker, as long as you thoroughly grease and line the pan, or you can use a slow cooker liner; this will make a flatter cake, depending on the size of your slow cooker, but it will still taste delicious.

4 Place the batter into the tin/liner and spread it out evenly. If you wish, you can cut an additional banana lengthways and put it on the top of the cake, as shown in the photo.

5 Place a tea towel under the lid as this helps to absorb any moisture. Cook on low for 3–4 hours or on high for 2–2½ hours until the cake is firm in the centre. Timings will vary depending on your machine. Older machines may cook more unevenly and can catch in places, in which case I would recommend cooking on low and using liners.

NUTRITIONAL INFORMATION PER SERVING

343 Kcals

9.2g fat

55g net carbohydrates

8.3g protein

INGREDIENTS

120g butter

100g light brown sugar

3 ripe bananas, mashed

2 eggs

225g self-raising flour

1 tsp cinnamon

1 tsp vanilla extract

60g walnuts, finely chopped

The slow cooker is so versatile – it is not just for casseroles and soups! I use it to make up spiced nuts, granola and stock. You can also make your own tomato sauce, which is excellent when making bolognese, lasagne or your favourite pasta dish.

STERILISE!

Before making preserves or chutneys, you need to sterilise your jars. You can do this in your dishwasher or you can use a more traditional technique, as described below.

1 Wash the jars thoroughly in warm, clean, soapy water, rinse and drain upside down on kitchen towel, then place them on a baking tray or directly onto an oven rack (if using the oven rack, take care when you remove them).

2 Place into a preheated oven at 100°C for 15 minutes.

3 After 15 minutes, turn the oven to its lowest setting to keep jars warm while you make your preserve or chutney. When removing the jars from the oven, place them onto an old newspaper or tea towel. Be careful not to touch the insides of the jars as you will contaminate them.

STORAGE

All the sauces in this chapter can be frozen. Alternatively, they can be stored in an airtight container in the fridge for up to a week. Chutneys in sterilised jars can be kept for up to three months in a store cupboard. Curds can last up to three months if kept in a refrigerator unopened, six weeks in a cool, dark place, but only about a week once opened. For this reason, I tend to pop curds into small jars to avoid wastage.

BONE BROTH/STOCK

INGREDIENTS

1kg bones (bone marrow, ribs, knuckles, etc.)

200ml apple cider vinegar

2 large onions, chopped into quarters

2 garlic cloves, cut into chunks

2 carrots, cut into chunks

2–3 sticks celery, cut into chunks

2 tsp mixed herbs

small handful fresh parsley (or 2–3 tsp dried)

2–3 bay leaves

2 tsp peppercorns

I include this bone broth/stock recipe in all of my books as it is a vital part of slow cooking. If you make your own stock it really is superior in taste/flavour, and much better for you than processed stock cubes. It is packed with minerals such as calcium, magnesium and phosphorus, as well as collagen, glucosamine and hyaluronic acid, and a wide range of vitamins. It helps support the digestive tract, boosts the immune system, reduces inflammation, strengthens the joints, hair and nails, and promotes healthy skin. Butchers are often happy to give away bones for you to use, so do ask them.

I store this in freezer bags as well as some large silicon ice-cube moulds. The freezer bags can be defrosted quickly by popping them, still sealed, into a bowl of water. I use the silicon moulds to pop out a few small stock 'ice cubes' to add to dishes such as a chilli or spaghetti bolognese.

1 If using meaty bones, place them in the oven and roast for 45 minutes to help release the flavours and nutrients. You can omit this step if you prefer.

2 Preheat your slow cooker following the manufacturer's instructions.

3 Place all the ingredients into your slow cooker and cover with water.

4 Cook on low for 24–48 hours.

5 You may want to remove any scum from the surface of the water occasionally. This is perfectly normal. I use a slotted spoon and just scoop it out.

6 When cooked, remove from the slow cooker and strain. It will form a layer of fat on the top once cooled and settled. Don't discard this – it can be used as cooking fat.

7 Place in a jar, freezer bag or even silicon ice moulds ready to use in your everyday savoury dishes.

SPICED RED ONION & SULTANA CHUTNEY

MAKES 2 JARS

This is a very easy savoury, sweet and spiced red onion chutney. It is delicious served with cheese on toast, on top of your favourite burger, or just as a tasty addition to your favourite salad or as a side with a curry. I also use it as a base for a red onion and goat's cheese tart. If you don't want the extra heat of the spices, you can omit them to create a standard sweet onion chutney. I store this in a sterilised jar in the fridge.

1 Preheat your slow cooker following the manufacturer's instructions.

2 Heat the oil in a sauté pan or, if you have a multi-cooker, use the sauté facility. Add the onions and butter. Cook until the onions are starting to soften and become more translucent.

3 Add the sugar, garlic, ginger and chillies, and stir well.

4 Add the cinnamon, star anise and bay leaves.

5 Place in your slow cooker and cook on high for 1 hour.

6 Add the remaining ingredients, except the seasoning, and cook for another 2 hours, or until the liquid has reduced, but not dried. Remove the cinnamon stick, star anise and bay leaves.

7 Season and store in the fridge until needed.

NUTRITIONAL INFORMATION PER SERVING

18 Kcals

0.5g fat

3.3g net carbohydrates

0g protein

INGREDIENTS

2–3 tbsp olive oil

500g red onions, sliced

20g butter

100g dark brown sugar

3 garlic cloves, diced

4cm piece fresh ginger, peeled and finely grated

3–5 red chillies, diced (deseed if you don't want it overly hot)

1 cinnamon stick

1 star anise

2 bay leaves

100g sultanas

1 tsp paprika

150ml red wine

75ml balsamic vinegar

seasoning, to taste

LEMON & LIME CURD

NUTRITIONAL INFORMATION
PER SERVING

39 Kcals

2g fat

4.2g net carbohydrates

0.7g protein

INGREDIENTS

100g butter

200g caster sugar

zest and juice of 3 large lemons (pips removed)

zest and juice of 3 limes (pips removed)

4 eggs

This is a variation on lemon curd that I now prefer as it has more of a citrus kick. It is delightful with toast, but I tend to use it more for my go-to breakfast, adding a large dollop to Greek yoghurt and blueberries. It is also delicious when combined with cream cheese and cream to create a lovely quick and easy mousse.

You will need a 1 litre pudding basin and tinfoil.

1 Place the butter, sugar, lemon and lime zest and juice in your pudding basin. Place in the slow cooker and turn to low. Pour boiling water into the slow cooker until it comes halfway up the basin.

2 Leave for 20 minutes. Remove from the slow cooker and leave to cool for 5 minutes. Keep the slow cooker on as you will be returning the basin to it shortly.

3 Beat the eggs and, while continuing to beat, pour through a sieve into the lemon/lime mixture.

4 Take a square of tinfoil larger than the top of your basin. Place it over the basin and seal well with string, making sure it is tied tightly.

5 Place the basin back into the slow cooker, keeping the temperature low. Add more boiling water around the basin, ensuring the water comes over halfway up the bowl.

6 Cook for 2–3 hours, stirring a couple of times to avoid any lumps (if you forget to stir and it goes lumpy or curdles, whisk well with a balloon whisk).

7 The curd should be thick enough to hold when poured from the back of a spoon, but not thick and lumpy.

8 Pour into your sterilised jars. Cover with a layer of parchment before sealing with the lids.

9 Keep refrigerated once opened.

MUM'S SEVILLE ORANGE MARMALADE

MAKES APPROX. 3 JARS

Traditionally, Seville oranges are used to make marmalade (these small, very sour oranges are in season at the beginning of the year). However, marmalade can be made from almost all citrus fruits, or a mixture of several. Why not try orange, orange and lemon, lemon and lime, or grapefruit? Clementines and satsumas will give a very sweet marmalade, more like a jam. Citrus peel takes a while to soften, so this recipe is ideal for the slow cooker.

1 Wash the fruit to get rid of any dirt or coatings.

2 Quarter the oranges and the lemon, and remove all the pith and the pips. Do this over a bowl or tray, to retain all the juice. All of the fruit is used when making marmalade, including the peel, pith and pips, as these help to give a good set.

3 Place the pith and pips into a muslin bag and tie tightly.

4 Pour any juice into the slow cooker and add the water.

5 Slice the peel to the required size – thick or thin, depending on your personal preference. This is best done on a chopping board with a sharp knife.

6 Place the peel into the cooker, lay the muslin bag on top and cook on high for 2–3 hours, stirring occasionally.

7 Once you are happy with the peel, turn off the slow cooker and allow to cool.

8 The next day, pour the mixture into a large saucepan, or a preserving pan if you have one. Heat until simmering. Add the sugar and stir until it has dissolved, then bring to the boil and boil rapidly for 10 minutes.

9 Test for setting by putting a teaspoon of the marmalade onto a cold plate. After 10 minutes gently push the liquid with your index finger. If small creases are made on the skin of the sample, it is ready to put into jars. If not, boil for a further 5–10 minutes and repeat the test until the correct consistency is achieved. Marmalade takes longer to set than other jams.

10 When set, pour into sterilised jars.

NUTRITIONAL INFORMATION PER SERVING

38 Kcals

0.6g fat

6.8g net carbohydrates

1.2g protein

INGREDIENTS

600g Seville oranges

1 large lemon

1 litre water

500g sugar (I use preserving sugar, but granulated can also be used)

NOTE

This is a two-step process, but if you want to speed things up, you can transfer the mixture into a large pan when you add the sugar and use on a hob, or, if you have a multi-cooker, just switch to sauté facility for the last stage, bringing to the boil/simmer. Please take care, though, as the mixture is very hot and will burn easily.

STRAWBERRY JAM

MAKES 3 JARS

NUTRITIONAL INFORMATION PER SERVING

22 Kcals

0g fat

5g net carbohydrates

0g protein

INGREDIENTS

1kg strawberries, hulled and sliced

1 tbsp lemon juice

400g preserving sugar

There is nothing like a good home-made jam. This is a recipe for a very simple strawberry jam, but you can use the same formula for raspberry if you prefer.

1 Preheat your slow cooker following the manufacturer's instructions.

2 Place all the ingredients into your slow cooker and combine. Don't worry if the mixture looks dry, the strawberries will release liquid as they cook.

3 Cook on low for 1½–2 hours.

4 Remove the slow cooker lid and continue to cook on low until you reach your desired consistency. It should be like a thick but fluid sauce.

5 When ready, place the jam into your sterilised jars. Leave to cool completely before popping on the lids. The jam will start to set a little more as it cools.

VARIATIONS

You can add some variety to this recipe. You can opt for half and half with another berry such as raspberry or blueberry. You can also opt for rhubarb, which works brilliantly with strawberry. You could add some brandy or Chambord raspberry liqueur, or, if you like herb flavours, you can add basil or tarragon, both of which work brilliantly with strawberry.

Index